# STEPS

## FOR IMPLEMENTING
## LOCAL AREA NETWORKS

303

# STEPS

## FOR IMPLEMENTING LOCAL AREA NETWORKS

### A Business Guide

**PETER CAUCHI**
**SUZANNE DENNISON**

**John Wiley & Sons**

Toronto · New York · Chichester · Brisbane · Singapore

**John Wiley & Sons Canada Limited**
22 Worcester Road
Rexdale, Ontario M9W 1L1

**Canadian Cataloguing in Publication Data**

Cauchi, Peter, 1955-
    STEPS for implementing local area networks
Includes bibliographical references and index.
ISBN 0-471-64045-X

1. Business - Data processing.  2. Local area
networks (Computer networks).  3. Business -
Communication systems - Data processing.
I. Dennison, Suzanne, 1951-   . II. Title.

HF5548.2.C38 1993       650'.0285'468    C92-095600-9

Printed and bound in Canada
10 9 8 7 6 5 4 3 2 1

# Trademarks

**Production Credits**

Designer:       Selwyn Simon
Page Layout:    Selwyn Simon
Printer:        John Deyell Company Ltd.

For Lauren Eden and Erin Dawn, for their hugs
and understanding, with love always

# CONTENTS

# PART TWO

. . . . . . . . . .
# Preface

Today more than ever before, businesses face the need to streamline and enhance their operations, and seek innovative ways of maintaining and increasing their competitive edge. Automated tools are one obvious solution. They offer uniformity, corporate standardization, and improved service and responsiveness. Ten years ago, the enhancement of operating efficiency involved general office automation and the implementation of various productivity tools on minicomputers and mainframes. Today, it encompasses work group integration and local area networks (LANs). LANs have become one of the fastest-growing areas of interest within the business community. Market analysts have predicted the greatest LAN growth to occur in 1992 - 1997.

Like any operational change in a business environment, a LAN implementation must be planned with care. The first critical stage is to make certain that the proposed change is appropriate. The next is to choose an effective, well-documented implementation methodology which can be easily understood by all concerned. The latter stage is essential for minimizing disruption to operations.

The personnel directly involved in managing a LAN implementation require an in-depth understanding of the implementation process. These people will, as a rule, be busy and short of staff, and have limited time to acquire the necessary expertise. *STEPS for Implementing Local Area Networks* is specifically designed for this market, providing solutions to the challenges of implementation before they become problems. Unlike most publications in the field, this book is oriented toward managers rather than a strictly technical audience. Whether you are a senior manager, a technical manager, a non-technical project manager, a LAN salesperson, or a supplier of LAN-related services, this publication offers an explicit and easy-to-follow approach to the implementation and documentation of a local area network.

STEPS is an acronym for Structured Transition and Engineering Planning System. The name means just what it says. STEPS is a clearly organized and extensively tested step-by-step methodology for planning your LAN implementation and carrying it out successfully.

For maximum ease of understanding and clarity, the book is divided into two main sections. Part One (Chapters 1 - 6) gives an overview of the STEPS process and briefly introduces some of its central components. The topics covered include the following:

- The language of local area networks. Familiarity with the terminology related to LANs is essential. Regardless of your functional role, your background, or your reasons for learning about LANs, you must first understand what a LAN is and does.

- A look at the people necessary to a LAN implementation team, as well as the skill sets they require

- General management guides to assist you in developing a needs analysis, application pilots, a cost-benefit analysis, and the strategic operational plans relating to security, back-up, disaster recovery, support, training, and finance

All these aspects of a LAN implementation are vital to its success. You may find that some of the tasks listed will involve more work than others, depending on such factors as your business environment, corporate information plans, and the size and scope of your implementation. However, they all should be included and related to your overall corporate strategy. Since you probably already know how to undertake some of these tasks, we have discussed them in terms of their relationship to LAN implementation, each in an appropriately titled chapter. Ultimately, the design of your LAN should reflect the factors specific to your business.

Part Two (Chapters 7 - 11) presents the STEPS process itself. Whatever your role in LAN implementation, this guide will provide both the general and the detailed information needed for understanding the implementation process. Once you acquire this knowledge, it is a short step to being able to adapt the process to your specific needs.

Chapter 7 reviews why and how to deal with project reporting, control, and accountability. These items are presented as a package of carefully developed STEPS: Tools — forms and reports designed to organize, document, and, if desired, automate all your information requirements for later use. One of the most valuable aspects of the STEPS process is that both tracking and accountability mechanisms are built into every stage of the implementation. That is, STEPS: Tools is completely integrated with the implementation process, furnishing the checks and balances required for a successful implementation.

Chapters 8 - 11 walk you through the STEPS process. We have adopted a four-phase approach to LAN implementation, each one covered in its own chapter. The following aspects of each phase are discussed:

• Each activity necessary, and who undertakes it

• The relevant control mechanism

• The deliverable(s), and where accountability lies

• The related detailed tasks

These chapters also describe the circumstances under which to use the STEPS: Tools, and how to combine the software with other material for project control and reporting.

Finally, to help you gain familiarity with the perhaps unfamiliar tools and terminology that you will encounter, a Glossary has been included at the end of the book.

Our objective in writing *STEPS for Implementing Local Area Networks* is to demystify what is widely considered to be a highly technical undertaking. The STEPS process provides direction, information, and practical tools related to important management concerns about LAN implementation. The STEPS: Tools software is designed to help you and the people you work with organize and consolidate LAN-related information in a consistent, audited manner. STEPS: Tools has been designed with Microsoft Project for Windows and DELRINA PerForm PRO, and may be obtained on floppy disk by means of the enclosed fulfillment card. Sample copies of all STEPS: Forms and Project Templates are included in the book.

After reading *STEPS for Implementing Local Area Networks*, you will know what a LAN is and what it does. You will understand the STEPS process. You will be able to relate issues to procedures and control mechanisms, and, with the tools provided, know how to customize STEPS for maximum effectiveness in your own business environment. You will also have the documentation essential for ongoing post-implementation service and support.

This publication is both a reference guide and a communication vehicle. It is explicitly designed to be a generic, vendor-independent approach to the tasks and issues involved in a LAN implementation. Regardless of either the scope of your LAN or its implementor — whether in-house staff or an outside party — you can hand *STEPS for Implementing Local Area Networks* and the STEPS: Tools software to your project leader, and be assured of a sound methodology and a reliable means of maintaining and measuring accountability throughout your LAN implementation.

# Acknowledgements

This book has benefited greatly from the assistance, wisdom, generosity, and support of many people: our editor, mentors, colleagues, friends, and family.

In particular, five people deserve special mention for the contributions they made to our work. To Bertha and Leslie Shvemar, there is no way that we can express enough gratitude for their encouragement and support. Suzanne owes special thanks to her father, Leslie, for her determination that the world was made to be explored and probed; to her mother, Bertha, for shaping her values; and to both for their personal examples of initiative, integrity, and the courage to challenge the unfamiliar. To Karen Milner, our editor at John Wiley & Sons, we are thankful for her immediate and continued enthusiasm, insightful criticism, and relentless effort in helping to get this book into print. To Julia Woods, also of John Wiley & Sons, who supported this book from the start, and was always there when we needed her input, we are grateful. To Brian Fraser, we are deeply grateful for his belief in our work, which was put into practice when we most needed it.

We also owe a special acknowledgement to three people without whom this book would not have been possible. We express gratitude to John Hylton of Borden & Elliot who, as a mentor and friend, has always been available over the years for discussion, comment, and referral. Peter is especially grateful to Eric Ross of Northern Telecom Inc. for working directly with him, giving real meaning to the word service, and demonstrating how effective senior management operates. Suzanne owes special thanks to Peter Herrndorf, who opened many doors and remains an approachable mentor.

Our last words of thanks happily go to Michael Hirsh and Elaine Waisglass, Gary and Lisa Maavara, and Janet-Lee and George Nadas who offered experience, comment, concern, and good food to keep us going.

# PART
# ONE

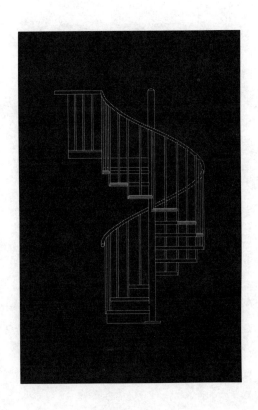

CHAPTER

# 1

# AN INTRODUCTION TO LANS
# AND THE STEPS PROCESS

· · · · · · · · · · · · · · · · · · · · · · · ·

## AN INTRODUCTION TO LANS
## AND THE STEPS PROCESS

Economic decline and increased globalization during the late 1980s and 1990s have led many organizations to re-evaluate their direction. There is a new emphasis on service, responsiveness, and productivity. There is also an awareness that more must be accomplished with less, and that cost-cutting must be an ongoing exercise.

These market conditions have given rise to several organizational trends. We will look at three of them: organizational responsiveness, restructuring, and the flourishing technology of distributed information systems. This discussion is by no means the final word on today's organizational issues. Rather, it serves to suggest how rapidly business practices are changing in the areas of accountability, processes and procedures, the requisite managerial and technical skills, and overall data management.

*Responsiveness*: To achieve present corporate goals and remain competitive for the future, organizations must be responsive to the needs of their clients or customers. Many businesses have come to realize that their success depends largely on the effectiveness of their planning and on their ability to cope with constant rapid change. They recognize that they must be more responsive at the level of their business units, and that current management processes and procedures must be altered. Their front-line people have to acquire additional skills and improved automated information tools.

*Restructuring*: Companies are restructuring in order to become more responsive to customer needs, moving areas of their planning and support responsibilities to the front line. In the process, they are changing in structure from large, centrally controlled units to smaller, distributed units. They are attempting to standardize their offerings, eliminate duplication of resources and services, increase their flexibility, and rationalize where business functions truly belong.

Transferring planning and control to smaller, distributed business units gives specific local user groups the power to develop and implement their own short-term — more responsive — tactical planning. It also calls for improved accountability, management, and technical skills in the individual units.

*Distributed information systems*: As organizations grow in size, they find that adopting a style of distributed — as opposed to centralized — information technology helps them remain competitive. The move from large, centrally controlled mainframe environments to smaller distributed systems such as minicomputers and LANs should lead to cost reductions. It should also encourage the development of more user-specific, practical, and successful applications.

The decentralization of certain information systems often serves as the catalyst for eliminating the duplication of resources and services, while simultaneously increasing the skill sets and responsiveness of front-line staff. This is not to say that all centralized systems vanish; large databases and accounting functions may continue to rest with a host computer. However, specific applications should be rationally reviewed on a regular case-by-case basis, in order to determine whether control should be managed in a centralized or distributed fashion. In addition, well-defined and well-designed communication lines should be developed for and between the central information technology group and all front-line business units.

The three trends summarized above are emerging in both private- and public-sector organizations. It must be emphasized that they do not dictate the elimination of mainframe environments. They do, however, suggest a change in orientation vis-à-vis the use of mainframe and LAN systems. This development raises numerous issues central to organizational management.

Both the issues and the way your organization chooses to respond to them will be laid out in its corporate strategic plan. This plan provides the rationale for any information technology planning undertaken by your organization, and is a necessary element in the design of a LAN implementation. Since every organization will have its own style and criteria for developing an information technology strategic plan, we do not intend to continue this discussion. It has been included here to restate our belief that, before you look at any technological solution, you must address how the proposed changes will affect your organization and the way it does business.

The rest of this chapter provides a brief look at what a LAN is and does, as well as an overview of the STEPS process. You may find parts of this discussion quite technical in nature. They may well be, but keep in mind as you read that you will probably not be the person who must perform the necessary tasks. Much of the work related to the implementation will be done by other parties: in-house technical staff, consultants, contractors, or vendors. The technical details are included to give you, as a manager (technical or otherwise), a good overall understanding of the STEPS process. Even when you have finished this book, it is unlikely that you will be able to take on such technical tasks as designing, wiring, or installing a LAN. You will, however, be aware of what each task entails, why it is required, what the related deliverable is, and who is responsible for completing the job.

# **L**AN BASICS

A **local area network** is formed by physically connecting several computers and related equipment, so that all the devices can communicate with one another without requiring a central processor. Specially designed control software allows the workstations to operate independently while sharing such resources as printers, faxes, disk drives, files, and application programs. A single system can consist of as few as two to ten workstations and a printer, or as many as a thousand workstations and hundreds of printers. The actual physical connections are accomplished with cable (e.g., twisted pair, coaxial cable, fibre optics), and a network interface card (NIC) inserted into each device connected to the network. Figure 1.1 shows the basic components of a simple LAN.

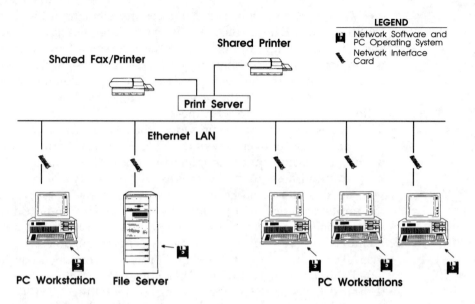

*Figure 1.1: Components of a Simple LAN*

Historically, the primary purpose of local area networks has been to provide interconnections among people and equipment. LANs offer electronic mail (E-mail), file sharing, and the sharing of printers and external communications services such as modems and dedicated lines. Depending on the LAN, connections vary in distance: within one room, throughout one floor of a building, or between floors to a shared resource such as a host or mainframe computer. A LAN may also be the connection to remote computing resources provided by a **wide area network** (WAN) — for example, between head office and branch offices.

A properly run LAN environment has both end users and LAN administrators. The latter are responsible for administrative and security controls at the work group level. In a small LAN of up to 20 users, there may be a single administrator. In a larger organization there will be several, each responsible for a particular work group, as well as a network supervisor having the broadest access to the network for general administration, security, and support.

The LAN administrator must obtain information about the matters listed below, and supervise them on a continuing basis:

- End user profiles: Descriptions of account set-ups, log-in procedures, security, and similar details, for each end user

- Security privileges and related resource access plans: Descriptions of dial-up connections and specific file and/or directory privileges; generally involve setting up passwords, establishing their regular expiry times, doing routine security audits, and so on

- System support and maintenance: Descriptions and routines for reporting problems, doing maintenance and back-up logs, providing continuing site documentation, establishing service and support agreements, and so on

At the most basic level, having access to a LAN means that you will no longer have to carry your floppy disk across the office to share information or a printer. At its best, sound administration and good system planning for a LAN will make it possible for all workers in your business to safely share information, programs, and peripheral equipment.

# LAN IMPLEMENTATION AND THE STEPS PROCESS

It might appear that to install a LAN and make it operational should be as simple as connecting a few PCs and printers with cable and adding some network version software. In fact, depending on the scope of the LAN, the variety of equipment involved, and the related applications, implementation can be quite a complex undertaking.

Too many organizations enter into a LAN implementation without understanding all the issues and details. As a result, key components affecting their daily business or the installation itself may be overlooked. Such businesses may find themselves in the undesirable position of being forced to deal with unexpected problems and conflicts, rather than with the tasks required for the implementation. Planning and using a systematic implementation process will make it possible for you to anticipate most problem areas and minimize office disruption during the introduction of the LAN.

Success throughout the delivery cycle of a LAN depends on a series of activities, from the establishment of corporate information requirements and the identification of user needs, to user acceptance and the arrangement of all necessary support mechanisms. Any LAN implementation benefits from the application of these principles of planning, analysis, and control.

The LAN implementation process described in this book is designed to conform with your corporate information technology strategic plan.

All corporate objectives, policies, and standards which will affect various steps of the process can therefore be reflected in any final system solution.

The STEPS process consists of four phases, as shown in Table 1.1: planning and design, installation preparation, the installation itself, and post-installation. As mentioned in the Preface, Chapters 8 – 11 each cover one phase of the STEPS process.

| Phase I Planning and Design | Phase II Installation Preparation | Phase III Installation | Phase IV Post-Installation |
|---|---|---|---|
| Project Start-up | Equipment Ordering | Site Installation | Orientation and Initial Support |
| Technical Requirements and Design | System Prototyping | Documentation Set-up (User Training) | Post-Installation Review |
| | Pre-configuration and Testing | | |
| Functional Design Review (Management Sign-off) | Site Preparation (LAN Administrator Training) | | Formal System Acceptance (Management Sign-off) |

*Table 1.1: The STEPS Process Framework*

## Phase I: Planning and Design

Phase I of the STEPS process is in many ways the most critical portion of the entire implementation. It is the longest and most involved, the stage that lays the foundation for all that is to come. The greater the effort committed to this phase of the project, the fewer the surprises and the less problematic the remainder of the implementation. During this opening phase, you select your project team, create lines of accountability, define organizational needs, and design your system solution. It is here that the STEPS: Forms and the STEPS: Tools software really come into play, helping you organize and document all information requirements in a consistent manner for later use.

Aside from management controls and authorizations, most activities in Phase I are undertaken by the project leader and designated team members. This phase of the STEPS process is examined in detail in Chapter 8.

At the completion of Phase I, you will have the following:

CHECK
LIST

✔ A **site inspection report** (SIR), which is a compilation of various STEPS: Forms describing the current work environment in both functional and physical terms

✔ A **system solution report** (SSR), which contains detailed descriptive information and specifications for the proposed solution design and its implementation. The documentation includes the strategic operational plans for such matters as security, back-ups, training, support, and disaster recovery. It serves to simplify future changes to the network and any related problem identification and resolution.

✔ A **site upgrade requirements report** (SURR), which details all the physical site requirements that must be addressed before installation, the costs involved, and target dates for completion of this work

✔ Authorization to implement your network solution

The first three of these are the key deliverables for Phase I of the STEPS process. They must all be reviewed and rationalized in light of management expectations. This is the point at which to address discrepancies and weaknesses in the solution. The preferred means for resolving any problems are application pilots and cost-benefit analyses. If such limited-scale tryouts or analyses are necessary, they should be done at this time, before Phase II. Application pilots and cost-benefit analyses are the focus of Chapters 4 and 5, respectively.

## Phase II: Installation Preparation

This phase follows the decision to proceed with implementation. It is now that the final preparatory work essential for a successful installation is done. In Phase II, you verify that the necessary equipment has been ordered, delivered, and tested, and that the related documentation has been recorded on the appropriate STEPS: Forms. You also arrange for your installation team and/or outside contractors to make any required upgrades to the LAN site. Finally, you verify that the LAN administrator has received the appropriate training.

When reading Chapter 9, which covers Phase II in depth, keep in mind that these activities are traditionally the responsibility of the technical members of the project team. It is they who must understand the terminology, undertake such necessary tasks as configuring and testing the servers and other equipment, and sign off on the completed preparations. Once all this work is finished, a memo is sent to site management indicating that the site is ready for the installation of the LAN. This memo, the key deliverable of Phase II, is added to the site upgrade requirements report in order to document approval to move on to Phase III.

## Phase III: Installation

The STEPS process is designed to ensure that LAN installation is swift and causes minimal disruption. Having methodically worked through both the planning and design phase and the installation preparation phase, you should find the installation and documentation of your LAN a relatively simple exercise.

At this point, the new equipment is in readiness, and the LAN site has undergone all required preparation. Phase III can be as straightforward as placing the servers in the appropriate locations, setting up the necessary physical connections, and installing software in the existing site workstations. With these tasks completed, all that remains is for the installation team to perform initial testing and check that all documentation is in order.

In practice, installations rarely work exactly as planned. However, the STEPS process, in concert with well-trained personnel, should furnish you with an accurate, up-to-date audit trail and all the documentation needed for dealing efficiently with unexpected difficulties.

## Phase IV: Post-Installation

This is the final stage of the STEPS process. It is time for the members of your project team to review their work with the LAN administrator and key end users, looking again at all written documentation, strategic operational plans, and preventive maintenance issues. The review covers the documentation and administrative procedures relating to such items as these:

- The back-up plan and back-up log

- The disaster recovery plan

- The support plan and network maintenance logs

- The training plan and LAN user guide

- The security plan and user set-ups

- Preventive maintenance procedures

- Procedures for resolving problems

The purpose of the review is to make certain that all documentation is understood, being used, and kept current.

It is also at this stage that the users have the opportunity to raise any questions and concerns about their new or changed LAN. They may do so at a single orientation session or several, as required. Extending the sessions over a longer period allows the users to be properly trained and site management to verify that all equipment is operating as anticipated. It also provides time for resolving any unforeseen problems.

Clearly, formal system acceptance and the completion of Phase IV should not occur until after at least one review session has been held. The period that should elapse before formal acceptance will vary with the complexity of the LAN — as well as with whom you ask! We believe that two to six months following installation is optimal. Formal system acceptance, which indicates that the LAN implementation is complete, is the final key deliverable in the STEPS process.

Once installation has been completed, the following should be true for every successfully implemented LAN:

- An administrator will have been selected from among the end users, and designated as LAN administrator.

- Training will have taken place or been scheduled for all users, administrative and otherwise.

- Users will fully understand and be capable of using the application tools they have been given.

With your LAN up and operational, it becomes a vital component of your business operation. As such, it must be monitored, managed, enhanced, upgraded, and so on. It is therefore essential to guarantee that all related documentation is maintained in a systematic manner. The STEPS process and the related STEPS: Forms and STEPS: Tools software will help you begin this continual management with an up-to-date history of your LAN and relevant documentation. Continuing to use STEPS will assist in making upgrades and maintaining documentation in the same organized way.

Now that you have read this summary of the STEPS process, you can turn to further information on the necessary activities, process charts or project templates, and samples of forms relating to each phase of implementation in Part Two (Chapters 7 – 11). In the balance of Part One, you will find planning guidelines to assist with the managerial tasks of developing a needs analysis, planning application pilots, designing cost-benefit analyses, and evolving customized strategic operational plans — all necessary and integral components of your LAN.

NEEDS ANALYSIS

• • • • • • • • • • • • •

# NEEDS ANALYSIS

One of the most significant pieces of work that you can undertake in a LAN implementation is a **needs analysis study**. Its purpose is to research your organizational needs and identify appropriate opportunities for change. In the context of LAN implementation, a needs analysis study should always be consistent with the existing corporate information technology plan, and be developed prior to making any decision that alters current organizational technology. In this way, all corporate objectives, policies, and standards are sure to be reflected in any final network solution.

However, this ideal is not always attained. As we noted in Chapter 1, today's competitive pressures are providing a powerful incentive for organizations to increase their productivity. Successful firms are responding by restructuring to become more dynamic, faster, and more flexible. They are changing their strategic directions and organizational structure in order to be more responsive to developments in the marketplace, changing political conditions, and the available talent pools and financial resources. As a result, a decision to restructure, distribute information systems, or implement a LAN (whether throughout the organization or otherwise) may be made before a needs analysis study is undertaken. In this approach, management attempts to short-circuit the change process by dictating an overall direction — here, a LAN implementation. Such a methodology is being used by increasing numbers of organizations.

The introduction of a LAN does more than open the door to increased productivity and efficiency; it also allows organizations to alter the way in which people interact and work together. It is therefore essential for the corporate information technology plan to examine these matters from an organizational perspective before you undertake a needs analysis study. It must be emphasized that, regardless of whether you undertake the study to define the detail of your system solution, or simply relate its responses to an already chosen organizational direction, it remains an essential component of any successful LAN implementation.

The needs analysis study serves two main functions. Its primary purpose is reviewing, identifying, and defining the precise functional needs of the end users, leading to a statement known as a **functional requirements specification document.** If your organization does not know or has not documented its present needs, then, despite the existence of a clear corporate information technology plan, it is in an undesirable and highly vulnerable position with respect to finding the right system solution. When handed a wide-open request for proposal, information technology vendors are likely to submit their solutions on the basis of generalized anticipated needs and industry norms. The usual results of this approach are proposals that either do not go far enough or are "overkill" and too costly.

The second function of the needs analysis study is to help you and other LAN users prepare for the inevitable changes associated with new office technology. The questions in the study are structured in such a way that, as they define their needs, the end users have the opportunity to re-examine their own functional roles and rethink their approaches to doing business. While this purpose may not seem as critical as the first, it is important for you to remain aware that prospective changes in the workplace may cause workers anxiety. The development of the needs analysis described in this chapter helps users recognize and become comfortable with the following facts:

- The implementation of a new system is actually taking place.

- This is a change, and they are a part of it.

- They will necessarily be affected.

The ability of users to become involved in reviewing and adjusting to any new system is vital to its successful introduction.

All too often, organizations fail to think about education and training until the end of an implementation, when the tools are already on individual desks. Starting implementation with a needs analysis study helps some of the users' avoidance and hesitation disappear, since teaching is built directly into the process.

The sections which follow discuss the stages of a needs analysis study from start to finish.

# S TART-UP

The first matters to address in doing a needs analysis study can be expressed as two questions: Who will lead the study? Who will be involved in the planning sessions? The ideal response to the first of these is to select a project leader who will be available to carry out the entire LAN implementation. In practice, however, this is not always possible. The STEPS process is therefore designed to allow anyone with the requisite skill set to take on the project leader's role once the needs analysis is complete. This flexibility lets you select the project leader from in-house personnel, consultants, contractors, or vendor representatives.

With regard to the second question: It is not necessary to select the entire implementation team at this time. If, however, the needs analysis study follows the decision to implement, then it is often useful to have the team in place so the members may take part in the study. Details on selecting a project team and on the skill sets needed by the members are given in Chapter 3.

# O RIENTATION

After the project leader has been selected, the best way to begin the needs analysis study is to hold an orientation session or a series of such sessions. Whether there is one session or several depends primarily upon the number of end users of the LAN. A rule of thumb is that each session should have no more than 20 participants. In many organizations, the user group is too large, or the users' needs too complex, to be properly dealt with in a single session. A possible solution under these circumstances is to select group representatives to attend the first session, then meet with other users in subsequent sessions.

The orientation session typically includes some senior-level managers, the information systems manager, and the project leader. The most senior manager present can use it as an opportunity to outline corporate objectives and confirm senior-level support. The project leader can present — in non-technical terms — the specific objectives of the needs analysis, identify and define user needs, and describe the general process involved in developing the requisite material. Then the participating users can ask any questions that come to mind. The information systems manager gauges the users' reception of the information they have learned.

At the close of the orientation session, a copy of the **functional requirements specification outline** is distributed to each participant, whether management or line staff. This survey is designed to make everyone aware of the information that should be compiled by the end of the planning sessions, which constitute the next stage of needs analysis. The outline provides a framework for helping to detail what the client needs the new system to do in terms of the functional requirements of the business. Each item is included to ensure that the corporate objectives, each business unit's specific objectives, and functional requirements relating to system needs are all met.

The people completing the outline should be encouraged to include not only things they see as essential, but also those they think would be "nice to have". They should respond to all points they consider relevant to their particular business area. The outline should ideally be completed — in writing — before the first planning meeting. If the participants do not have sufficient time for this (as is often the case), then, at the very least, they should come to that meeting prepared to table their perspectives and rationales on functional requirements.

You should not expect the responses to be complete or perhaps even accurate. Fine-tuning will occur later, under the guidance of the project leader. The intent here is to encourage the participants to begin thinking about and questioning the issues related to implementation, before the first planning session. Subsequent discussion of this exercise will give the project leader a clear indication of the level at which each user is operating. This, in turn, will make it possible to better address the users' needs in future sessions.

## Functional Requirements Specification Outline

1. Describe the primary purpose and business function to be addressed by the new LAN system as it relates to your job (e.g., in the areas of

financial reporting, sales tracking, inventory management, scheduling, and the like).

2. Describe (a) how this function relates to the organization's overall operation and (b) how your department relates to other departments of the organization. (An organizational chart is often helpful here.)

3. List (a) the key objectives relating to this function and (b) how the function relates to your department's business objectives.

4. List the major functional areas you anticipate will be affected by the LAN, and describe in general terms what you should be able to do if it succeeds in addressing your needs in the areas of information capture, management, inquiry, reporting, and so on.

5. Itemize the specific business information that must be maintained and managed.

6. List your information access and reporting needs: What information most often has to be accessed? What presentation media should be used — printed reports, general inquiry screens? How should the information be organized as regards content and format?

7. Describe the normal business cycles of the organization, as well as the specific information needs during those cycles: fiscal year end, planning dates, fund-raising campaigns, sales initiatives, government dates, and so on.

8. Give details about your business information distribution needs, that is, to whom and how the information should be made available. (For example, some month-end information may be needed by your finance, marketing, and/or research departments.)

9. Describe the system's required operational characteristics, appearance, and flow; that is, how you want the system to feel, look, and work. In your description, make reference to menu screens, function keys, the content and hierarchy of the screens, graphic user interfaces (GUI), and the like.

***********************

The last item in the functional requirements specification outline is related to the definition of organizational policies and standards. It is anticipated that this information will be provided by your information systems group, and will consider all the points above in light of accepted organizational policies, objectives, and standards as defined in the corporate information technology strategic plan. For example, client-server architecture may be a strategic information systems standard. Use the information systems detail inquiries which follow to determine what the criteria may include.

## Information Systems Detail Inquiries

1. List the primary applications and/or application improvements that the system must perform.

2. List the end users, including the following details about them:

   - What equipment do they currently have access to — terminals, PCs, printers, external or remote computers?

   - Where will the users be located?

3. Itemize where the existing equipment is to be located, and who will use it.

4. What kind of environment will the equipment be going into — a computer room, a climate-controlled office, a hostile environment?

5. Are power outlets available in the planned location of the equipment?

6. How will the equipment be connected?

   - Are existing telephone wires in place and adequate?

   - Is there a need to string new wire?

   - Are wiring channels available in the ceiling or floor?

7. List all the available types of telephone cable and connectors, e.g., twisted pair, coaxial cable, fibre optics, etc.

8. Describe all anticipated changes in the users' environment.

9. What organizational standards must be considered in designing the solution?

   - Is there a standard spreadsheet, database, word processor?

   - Is there a standardized data communications scheme?

   - Is there a standard for PCs, printers, terminals, computer manufacturers, and so on?

10. List all LAN technology standards, e.g., ethernet, token ring, etc.

11. List all protocol standards, e.g., TCP/IP, etc.

12. Identify how the organization is likely to administer the system. Are the existing personnel and skill sets adequate, or will additional help be needed?

13. How will the success of the implementation be evaluated? Do criteria for this exist, or will they need to be developed so that the organization may perceive a successful implementation?

# P LANNING SESSIONS

The purpose of the planning sessions is to assess what the users already have, what they need, and what they might want. To this end, the preliminary responses to the functional requirements specification outline are examined at the meetings. The organization's functional structure is also scrutinized, to focus the users' responses on the following matters:

- Reporting lines in the organization's structure

- Identification of job functions, that is, job descriptions, roles, and responsibilities

- Possible changes in job functions resulting from the implementation (For instance, providing direct information access to others may alter existing roles.)

- Impressions of existing and anticipated problems and opportunities in such areas as security and the skill sets needed for ease of use

A typical tendency is to try to speed up the investigative process. While this may have no repercussions on the solution chosen, it is generally more effective to take the time to educate your personnel. Simply splitting up the planning sessions and the related tasks lets the users gain familiarity with them but does not unacceptably extend the targetted completion date. The extra time spent is worth it in the long run, since it accomplishes the following:

- It helps the uninitiated understand that detailing their roles and responsibilities vis-à-vis others and their own information requirements is more complex than they might have imagined.

- It allows the users to start rethinking their own functional needs or roles, placing them in a broader context.

- It encourages the users to become actively involved in and take ownership of the STEPS process.

Many LAN experts suggest the use of "champions" as prime user group co-ordinators or representatives, to expedite the planning process. In this context, a **champion** is a non-systems person who demonstrates greater-than-average interest in and aptitude for the use of computer tools. We feel that this approach may be effective, particularly in large organizations where champions often excel at collecting information and introducing the uninitiated to systems technology. However, champions are rarely skilled enough to effectively help other end users come to terms with their functional and cross-functional business relationships and needs. We generally recommend that the project leader or another team member, as well as relevant user group management, be involved in all planning sessions with end users.

## The Initial Planning Session

The initial planning session is primarily intended to allow the session leader to gauge the working level of the participants and to familiarize them with the implementation process. (The session leader is not necessarily the same person as the project leader.) The leader reviews the functional requirements specification outlines, and relates the information they contain to the material that will ultimately be required by the people who will design the new system (probably the project team).

The first planning meeting is the time for the session leader to give explanations, build understanding, and increase the participants' comfort level. It is *not* the time to finalize the material in the outline, since most participants will not yet be able to do so accurately. This will take place in later sessions. If your group of end users is fairly sophisticated, you may not consider it necessary to spend much time on easing them into the process. However, it is our experience that doing so helps avoid misinterpretation and problems later on.

Another task for the session leader is to have the users take a step back and draw a corporate or divisional chart outlining the functional areas or business units which are relevant to them. Figure 2.1 shows an example drawn from one firm with which we have worked.

The figure focuses on one major functional area or business unit within the organization, Community Development and Public Membership, and illustrates the various related functional areas within it. The core group is at the left, under the main heading. On the right are listed the business units that are involved with, but peripheral to, the core

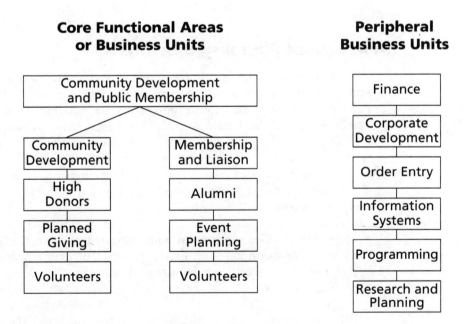

*Figure 2.1: Sample Organizational Chart*

group. These need not be listed in any particular order. It should be understood that in a large organization or one with complex needs, each unit is just one functional area among many.

The session leader should caution the participants to resist the natural temptation to focus on the detail of what they know best. It is important for them to recognize and understand overall organizational needs and objectives first of all. For instance, to return to the example in Figure 2.1, the users should examine the corporate information technology plan, then the global functions of Community Development and Public Membership itself, before zeroing in on the specifics of, say, Event Planning. The session leader also has the task of collating the information generated during this activity.

Once these general matters are sorted out, each participant can go on to state his or her individual functional objectives and needs. It works well to let the planning group adjourn in order to reconsider which peripheral business units ought to be included in the ongoing investigation. This marks the end of the initial planning session. The interlude gives the users an opportunity to absorb the new way of looking at their own organizational functions. The break between planning sessions does not have to be lengthy, but it is essential if the needs analysis is truly to begin the education and ownership process.

## Subsequent Planning Sessions

When the planning group reconvenes, the users' first task is to make and confirm any necessary changes to the organizational chart. Next, individuals are assigned the responsibility for detailing, in writing, the needs of a particular business unit. This exercise is in keeping with the overall objective of accountability inherent in the STEPS process. Each written assessment should relate to the functional requirements specification outline, and each participant should sign his or her version.

The following points about the current system should be included in each assessment:

- How closely does the system address the stated functional requirements? (For example, the finance department may require monthly statements to reconcile accounts and is currently relying on paper reports to do so.)

- What functional areas could be improved, and how? (For example, you may wish to give the finance department direct access to the data it needs from another department; or you may wish the system to be accessible by multilingual screens.)

- What are the key constraints or limitations of the present system? (For example, the paper reports now used by the finance group may not provide enough detail for proper accounting; an English-only system may restrict hiring.)

To aid the participants with this activity, the session leader would do well to provide them with a customized needs assessment matrix such as Table 2.1. You will likely find much of the terminology used in the table fairly straightforward. If, however, the users are unfamiliar with any of it, the session leader can supply the necessary explanations. Each participant should be sure to do the following:

CHECK
LIST

✔ Supply his or her name, title, department, and functional role on the completed matrix, as well as the date. (For example, David Nadas, Manager, High Donors, co-ordinating revenue generation, 17/8/93)

✔ Address all relevant items in the Functional Needs column.

✔ Mark N/A on the matrix for any item that is not relevant.

Once the participants have completed their matrices, there should be enough material for the session leader to prepare a summary. This information should be representative of each business unit and reflect the items in the functional specification requirements outline. As an example, let us turn again to David Nadas, the High Donors manager whose functional role is co-ordinating revenue generation. Two specific system requirements are related to his business function. The first is improving access to client information histories, to allow for more proactive marketing of services. The second is improving and increasing access to credit card information, to improve the processing of sales activities. The outcome of the summarization will be a written account of your organization's key business needs. The final system requirements specification will be based on each participant's written assessment.

On the basis of the summary, the planning group can go on to assess the current system in light of the functional needs expressed. A detailed review is needed to ensure that all the required information is included.

Next, a project team member conducts individual surveys assessing the skill set of each end user. If your organization is large, user group

| Category | Functional Needs |
|---|---|
| **General Needs** | Summarize or describe your overall objectives, your job or group functions, and what you need the system to do. |
| **Business Initiatives and Functions** | List current and planned business initiatives and functions.<br>What are their main objectives?<br>When and where do they take place?<br>Who is responsible for them?<br>How is information about this organized, and how should it be organized?<br>How do business initiatives and functions relate to the information system?<br>Should the information system be tied into them? |
| **Data Capture** | What data need to be captured?<br>Who is responsible for doing this, and where are these people located?<br>What are the sources of data? (e.g., computer, phone, data entry, etc.) |
| **Access to Information** | What information do you need to access? (e.g., databases, financial records, pre-authorized accounts, credit information, etc.)<br>How do you want the information to be made available to you? (e.g., inquiry screens, reports, file transfers, etc.)<br>What capabilities do you need with respect to this information? |
| **Screen Inquiry** | How many inquiry screens do you need?<br>If you were to name each, what would you call them?<br>What information needs to be on each screen?<br>Who will do the inquiry?<br>Will inquiries be scheduled or on demand?<br>What screen capabilities do you need here? (e.g., update, read only, sort, print screen, mail merge, etc.) |

*Table 2.1: Needs Assessment Matrix*

| Category | Functional Needs |
|---|---|
| **Reporting** | How many different reports do you need? If you were to name each, what would you call them? What information needs to be in each report? Who will generate reports? Will reports be scheduled or on demand? Do you need the ability to create or customize reports on an *ad hoc* basis? |
| **Information Ownership** | Do you need to have ownership of specific information? (e.g., master files, databases, financial material, etc.) If so, why? |
| **Archiving** | What needs to be archived? After what period should archiving occur? Where will archived information be stored ? How will the archives be organized? How is this material to be retrieved with respect to schedules, medium, and so on? Whom do you expect to be responsible for archiving and retrieval? |
| **Security** | Have you any special security needs with respect to certain information or programs? (Itemize as open file, read only, write only, create, delete, search and modify, execute only, copy only.) |
| **Global** | What capabilities and/or features do you need across the system? (e.g., multilingual input, cross-referencing, indexing, etc.) |
| **Other** | Discuss any other areas of concern which are not mentioned above. |

*Table 2.1: Needs Assessment Matrix (continued)*

managers may have to assist. The result is an accurate profile of the user community's training needs in such areas as computer-related experience, applications usage, and skill levels.

The **end user profile worksheet** provided with STEPS: Tools acts as an outline for determining individuals' computer usage needs and experience levels. Its detailed nature is essential to the later development of an effective system solution and a rollout plan — including a training plan — for each group of end users. Figure 2.2 gives an example of a completed end user profile worksheet.

Various seemingly unresolved functional issues tend to surface at this stage of the process. Common examples include the following:

- Access: Many different groups may need to access certain data directly.

- Ownership or control: The originator of information generally wants authority over access to it, but multi-departmental applications may have more than one originator.

- Accountability: An effective information system can have only one assigned accountable owner.

While the planning sessions provide a good forum for airing concerns about such matters, they are not the place for resolving them. Management is responsible for the resolution of these issues. It is therefore important to make certain that management is both aware of and in a position to deal with all major discrepancies in functional business issues before the planning sessions come to an end.

Once these concerns have been dealt with, a consensus approach is used to ascertain that all group goals and other necessary items have been covered. All items are given a general ranking at a final planning session. Once again, the participants are required to sign off — this time on the completed, agreed-upon material. The official sign-off indicates that the information to be included in the final document truly reflects the consensus reached.

The information systems group should have participated in the needs analysis study from the very beginning. If for some reason this is not the case, its members must now review the ranking of items. This exercise guarantees that all the seemingly minor but critical information system details are taken into account before the final functional requirements specification document is written. In addition, the participation of

# End User Profile Worksheet

Name: George Merek         Phone Ext #: 2883        Ref ID: EUP - 9301010001

Location: 2A10                                Originator Name (Print): Erin Dawn

                                                Signature:

Job Classification: Management                  Date Completed:93/07/21

## Experience

### Workstation Environment

| System Type | Environment | Very Experienced | Somewhat Familiar | Little/No Experience |
|---|---|---|---|---|
| PC386 | DOS | | | ✓ |
| | Microsoft Windows | ✓ | | |
| XYZ Mainframe Term Type 1 | MAINOS | | ✓ | |
| | XYZOFFICE | ✓ | | |
| | | | | |
| | | | | |
| | | | | |
| | | | | |

### Application Software

| Type of Software | Product Name/Version | Experience (Yrs) | Very Experienced | Somewhat Familiar | Little/No Experience |
|---|---|---|---|---|---|
| Word Processor | WordProcess 5.1 | 3.0 | ✓ | | |
| Accounting - Accounts Payable | AcctPayXX.YYY | 1.0 | ✓ | | |
| Groupware - Office Productivity | XYZOfficePRO | 3.0 | ✓ | | |
| | | | | | |
| | | | | | |
| | | | | | |
| | | | | | |

*Figure 2.2: End User Profile Worksheet*

the members enlists their support. The information systems detail inquiries survey on pages 22 – 23 gives examples of the information they must include. It is not essential for you to understand all the technical details involved here. However, you should take time to go over the information systems detail inquiries to become aware of the matters that your technical staff has to deal with.

Now the functional requirements specification document can be written up. If your organization is large, the document will be compiled from several business units' studies, which, depending upon time and resources, may be undertaken concurrently. It is then submitted for approval to the management group responsible. The final stage in your needs analysis study is complete.

The functional requirements specification document is a good foundation on which to build external sourcing documents such as these:

- **Request for information** (RFI): A formal request for specific information relating to products, support, and services

- **Request for quotation** (RFQ): A formal request for pricing related to products, support, and services

- **Request for proposal** (RFP): A formal request for a detailed proposal, including firm pricing, to address the specific requirements at hand

The document will also help you determine the direction and scope of the project to be undertaken — whether an upgrade to the existing system can meet your requirements, or a new system must be sought out and implemented. The functional requirements specification document is vital to the successful technical design phase of any implementation. You can learn more about how this information is used from Chapter 8.

THE PROJECT TEAM

• • • • • • • • • • • • • • •

# THE PROJECT TEAM

Choosing a project team according to the STEPS process is central to the success of any LAN implementation. Since each LAN will vary in size and complexity depending upon the organization for which it is designed, the people who actually implement it play a critical role. The project team is the group from which your business will obtain assurance that each phase of the STEPS process is being handled in an organized, responsive, and fully accountable manner. This chapter defines the various roles and responsibilities of the project team, the requisite skill sets of the members, as well as the schedule according to which they are typically selected.

You may find that some of the descriptions in this chapter are couched in fairly technical terms. This is essential, since those who are directly involved in the LAN implementation need a precise reference document detailing their skills and tasks. Keep in mind that undertaking these tasks will not necessarily be your responsibility. You do not, for example, need to know what a server is in order to be aware that the installation specialist is accountable for sign-off on its configuration. However, to ease your curiosity and any concerns you might have about such information, refer to the Glossary for definitions of technical terminology.

Before turning to specifics about the project team, you will find it useful to be aware of the range of its members' tasks:

CHECK
LIST

✔ Assessing users' needs and site requirements

✔ Developing an implementation plan tailored to your organization

✔ Designing the system most appropriate for your organization's needs

✔ Developing all necessary strategic operational plans

✔ Obtaining all approvals and authorizations needed in order to acquire the system

✔ Training the users to be prepared for change and for coping with change

✔ Readying the site for LAN installation

✔ Installing the LAN

✔ Integrating the LAN into the existing business environment

## S ELECTING THE PROJECT TEAM

There are many ways to select and organize your project team. Some organizations go to the extent of mapping individual psychological assessments against project requirements. Such elaborate methods are rarely used, however. The contemporary work environment seldom offers the luxury of the time they demand, and organizations simply turn to using available resources.

The selection of the core project team depends on three major criteria. Of primary importance are the skill sets required for the implementation. Next are the time commitments that all team members will have to make. The final factor is the availability of in-house systems resources, which a small or mid-sized business might not even possess.

Most organizations prefer the project team to be composed of people from the resident information systems group. However, it is often the case that line staff do not have the time to undertake an implementation.

The obvious solution, and the one we have found most effective, is to draw your team members from a range of sources. It is common for a project team to consist of in-house information systems staff, outside consultants, contractors, service company representatives, and vendor representatives. A team will frequently work together with selected champions from key user groups. Champions are also referred to as "prime user group co-ordinators" throughout this book. They are most often assigned to the position of LAN administrator, as you will see later in the chapter.

Regardless of how capable your people are and how much time they have available, there are certain tasks in any LAN implementation for which it is advisable to rely on external sources. Certain areas of LAN implementation call for expertise that will not generally be needed by your organization once the LAN is in place:

- Building cable installation: This is normally contracted to outside service companies.

- The development of highly specialized areas such as information security, disaster planning, training, etc.: Many large consulting firms and service companies offer expertise on these matters.

- Vendor selection: Consulting firms are often brought in to undertake or advise on this process.

- Implementation project management: In small to mid-sized implementations (up to 50 users), the vendor is often required to perform this function as part of the sale. In large implementations, where the task is a lengthy, full-time commitment, it is often necessary to bring in an outside company.

Depending on the size of the implementation, the project team members plan the project and carry out the associated tasks. They do so either directly or by delegating assignments throughout the organization or to outside parties. No matter how the tasks are completed, maintaining accountability within the structure of the team is paramount. The team should hold weekly status review sessions to report on the project, in order to make sure it is on course and on schedule. The project leader uses these meetings for project tracking, discussing upcoming events, and dealing with any unresolved difficulties.

## Timing the Selection of the Project Team

You saw in Chapter 2 that the STEPS process begins with needs analysis, and that this study commences with the selection of the project leader. Depending on both the size of the needs analysis study and available resources, the project team may or may not also be chosen at this time. In general, if the study is to be a first step in examining and re-evaluating business needs, most organizations will have the project leader undertake the study (providing support as needed) but refrain from selecting the project team until a decision to act is approved. This is particularly true of large organizations in which functional needs and/or the decision-making process can be quite complex. It is also a reasonable approach, inasmuch as the core team's skill sets may vary greatly, as shown in the results of the needs analysis.

On the other hand, if project start-up follows a proactive management directive to move ahead with a new system — as more often happens — it is wise to select both the project leader and the project team at this time. Results are usually better if you are able to work with the same team throughout the implementation.

Regardless of the timing of its selection, the project team's fundamental role is to guarantee that your organization's LAN implementation is handled in a structured, systematic, and accountable manner from the very outset. As soon as the project team is in place, the project leader holds a planning session with team members to organize and assign individual involvement. The four phases of the STEPS process — planning and design, installation preparation, installation, and post-installation — are broken down according to detailed project tasks to which individual accountabilities and target dates are assigned. At the same meeting, other administrative requirements and resources may also be discussed and added to the project. The possibilities here include clerical support or additional in-house functions for such work as technical design. Each team member is expected to sign off on assignments to verify acceptance of responsibility, as at all stages of the STEPS process.

## ATTRIBUTES OF THE PROJECT TEAM

A successful implementation is predicated on project team members who have demonstrated their technical skills and their ability to both deliver results and accept responsibility. The team's collective knowledge base should cover the following:

- Proven project management skills and organizational knowledge related to user groups' needs and concerns

- The ability to get vendors to work for your organization

- Sound knowledge of any equipment at the site with which the new LAN may have to be integrated, such as corporate mainframe and network backbone systems

- Thorough understanding of all LAN operating systems (e.g., Microsoft LAN Manager, Novell Netware) involved in the implementation

- Proficiency with LAN operating system installation, including integration and interoperability with dissimilar platforms

- Proficiency with LAN technologies (e.g., token ring, ethernet) used in the implementation, including design, installation, testing, and repair

- Proficiency in the detection and repair of hardware malfunctions

As mentioned earlier, your final project team is likely to be comprised of information systems personnel, in-house champions, and members of outside organizations. The following roles are vital to the success of the implementation: project leader, technology advisor, installation specialist, trainer, project administrator, and LAN administrator. Each is discussed in a separate section below. Whatever their present line positions, both the project leader and the team members are assigned specific roles in accordance with their individual strengths and skills sets.

A good approach is to organize the team into two functional levels, the upper level relating to project management and administrative skills, and the other to technical and support issues. This two-tiered organization is represented in Figure 3.1, on the next page.

The size of the project team will vary with the scale of the LAN implementation. Small sites may have a single team member filling several roles, such as technology advisor, installation specialist, and project administrator. A complex implementation may require several team members for covering all the tasks related to a single role. For example, as many as five installation specialists may be necessary.

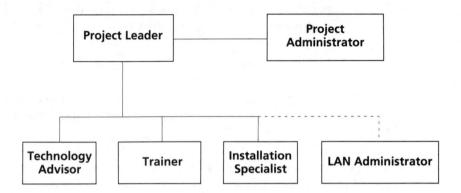

*Figure 3.1: Structure of the Project Team*

## Project Leader

The project leader is responsible for overall project organization, control, and reporting. This individual will have extensive experience in managing similar information systems implementations, and be selected on the basis of proven technical management skills rather than technical know-how. This distinction in skill sets is vital to the project team's success.

The project leader's primary function is to provide general guidance on both technical and non-technical matters relating to the implementation. He or she must make sure that all tasks are performed and completed at the proper time and in the correct order, according to all commitments and approved project plans. To achieve this goal, the project leader must maintain contact not only with senior management, team members, and end users, but also with many external resource people. Managing outside personnel can be particularly difficult, since their priorities cannot be directly controlled. For while the implementation is of utmost importance to your business, the priorities of outside resource people will change throughout the project.

The project leader should accomplish the following:

CHECK
LIST

✔ Direct both technical and non-technical aspects of the project

✔ Ensure that all stated needs and recommendations are consistent with the corporate information technology plan

✔ Organize and manage all available internal and external resources, such as participating departments, outside contractors, and non-performing team members

The project leader requires the following skill set:

- The personal qualities of being a tactician and task oriented

- Experience as a project manager; prior functioning at a management level

- Thorough knowledge of automated project management tools

- Demonstrated hands-on experience in an important role in a similar implementation, or at least in the role of technical advisor on a similar project

- Broad experience in dealing with vendors; ideally, previous contact with related information technology vendors

- Good working knowledge of the technology to be implemented (We stress again, however, that the project leader does not have to be a technology specialist.)

- Good oral and written communication skills

## Technology Advisor

This team member is responsible for ensuring that the client's needs are met and the physical site is prepared for the transition. Depending upon the size of the project, several technology advisors may be needed.

If the entire project team is selected at project start-up, the technology advisor will often work with the project leader to co-ordinate the first planning sessions and direct the needs analysis study. If not, the technology advisor enters the process when the work on technical requirements and design commences.

In either case, the technology advisor's first task is usually to investigate the users' proficiency and training requirements by means of the end user profile worksheets. Then comes the assessment of the physical site. On small implementations or a simple upgrade, the technology advisor may perform these tasks independently; on large, complex projects, he or she will likely combine forces with such support groups as the technical design, technical documentation, and training departments of the organization. When working with these support groups, the technology advisor must bring to bear his or her detailed knowledge of the end users, and skills in analysis and applications. For example, the technology advisor may perform the site surveys, then work with the technical design group to develop a design recommendation. Likewise, he or she may work with the training department to develop the site training plan. Whether the technology advisor performs these tasks independently or with the co-operation of some support group, he or she has accountability for the deliverables.

The technology advisor should accomplish the following:

CHECK
LIST

✔ Develop design recommendations, including system prototyping

✔ Develop the site training plan

✔ Furnish all related written documentation

✔ Supply presentation material for orientation sessions and technical recommendations

The technology advisor requires the following skill set:

- The personal quality of being able to cope with details

- Strong analytical and planning skills

- Well-developed capabilities in devising questionnaires and interviewing clients

- Good oral and written communication skills

- Strong capabilities in documentation and reporting

- Sound knowledge of LAN technology, cabling systems, and the building's electrical power design, as well as LAN installation

- Experience in the integration of dissimilar computing architectures

- Sound knowledge of related information technology design and support

- In-depth knowledge of related business applications

## Installation Specialist

The installation specialist installs the LAN hardware and software and integrates the new system with existing technology. For instance, if the existing facilities are a mainframe or minicomputer, all new equipment must be tied in so that the entire system operates as a whole.

Under the guidance of the project leader and the technology advisor, the installation specialist is responsible for pre-configuration and testing, as well as the installation itself. If any team member is to be drawn from the vendor community, these requirements make the installation specialist the most likely candidate.

The installation specialist should accomplish the following:

CHECK
LIST

✔ Install and configure the servers

✔ Format and set up workstation hard disks

✔ Create workstation shells for both new and existing equipment, allowing individual PCs to become part of the network

✔ Test all equipment and the network to verify that everything is operating correctly

The installation specialist requires the following skill set:

• Installation certification from the LAN vendor of choice; related vendor experience a definite asset

• Demonstrated experience in LAN installation, testing, and repair

• Sound knowledge of LAN technologies

• Proficiency in cabling system installation and testing techniques

## Trainer

The trainer, as the title suggests, is responsible for putting together the detailed training plan which will familiarize the users with the new system. The trainer also addresses any technical questions that may arise during training sessions. The scale of the implementation dictates whether the trainer will be required to provide post-installation network hardware and software support as well.

Depending upon the available resources, the trainer's role may be filled by in-house personnel — wholly or in part — or by outside training consultants. In the former case, the most likely source for the trainer is the systems department of your organization, because of the requirement to respond to technical inquiries. Even if an external training agency is commissioned, it will still be necessary for the project team to assign a trainer to ensure that all training material conforms to the approved training plan and meets management expectations regarding quality and price. In the latter case, the trainer's role is often filled by the technology advisor, who is responsible for seeing to the development of the training plan.

The trainer should accomplish the following:

CHECK
LIST

✔ Establish the details of the content of the training plan

✔ Develop handout and presentation material

✔ Deliver training material

✔ Supply refresher training for LAN administrators on a continuing basis

The trainer requires the following skill set:

- Extensive training experience

- Training certification from the LAN vendor of choice

- Broad knowledge of networking concepts

- Excellent oral and written communication skills

- Strong analytical and planning skills

- Experience in word processing and desktop publishing

## Project Administrator

The project administrator's main tasks are to act as the executive assistant to the project leader and to provide administrative and clerical support for the team members. All important correspondence, memos, forms, and reports related to the implementation are channelled through the project administrator for logging, filing, and distribution.

The importance of the project administrator, like that of many support staff members, is often overlooked. One of the most valuable aspects of the STEPS process is that it simplifies the auditing and documentation of all activities related to LAN implementation. The project administrator plays a critical role in  maintaining this audit trail.

The project administrator should accomplish the following:

CHECK
LIST

✔ Handle word processing

✔ Develop and maintain forms

✔ Do filing

✔ Manage general correspondence

✔ Distribute information as required

The project administrator requires the following skill set:

• The personal qualities of being thorough, organized, and capable of coping with details

• Strong administrative skills

• Proficiency with the organization's standard word processing software package

• Experience with software for developing and managing forms

## LAN Administrator

The responsibility for all day-to-day operations of the network rests with the LAN administrator. This team member also assists the end users and serves as a liaison between them and the LAN support staff.

The LAN administrator is chosen from the user community. In many cases, the position is filled when a champion emerges from among the end users during the early stages of implementation. As a result, the LAN  administrator, more than any other team member, is likely to lack LAN experience. It is therefore highly important to examine carefully the skill set and training requirements of this team member. As mentioned earlier, there may be more than one LAN administrator, depending on the scope of the implementation.

The LAN administrator should accomplish the following:

CHECK
LIST

✔ Monitor daily network operations

✔ Do regular back-ups of the system, both daily and on a longer-term basis

✔ Handle general system clean-up, such as the removal of old accounts and file directories

✔ Help users with minor problems, as determined in the support plan

✔ Maintain users' access rights and privileges

✔ Act as liaison between users and support staff

The LAN administrator requires the following skill set:

• The personal qualities of being thorough, organized, and capable of coping with details

• Strong administrative skills

• Proficiency in word processing

• Experience in managing forms, in both printed and electronic media

\*\*\*\*\*\*\*\*\*\*\*\*\*\*\*\*\*\*\*\*\*\*\*

Having read this chapter, you should have a good grasp of the tasks associated with LAN implementation and the skill sets required of the people who will perform those tasks. You are therefore ready to select your project team. Once you have done so, the information in Chapter 8 about Phase I of the STEPS process, planning and design, will help you in overseeing the matters related to implementation management, including lines of communication, resource requirements, accountability, and project scheduling.

APPLICATION PILOTS

# CHAPTER 4

## APPLICATION PILOTS

An **application pilot** is essentially a testing ground for unproven information technology. It generally comes into play during the planning and design phase of the STEPS process, after all possible planning has been done. At this time, the project team will have completed the first two activities in Phase I, project start-up and technical requirements and design. The team will also have issued the second key deliverable of the implementation, the system solution report. This document consists of the specifications for the proposed solution design.

The natural tendency is for many organizations, having come this far, to push forward with implementation. It is critical, though, to recognize that any proposed solution, however well researched, reflects anticipated results and benefits. Its design is necessarily based only on predicted needs. As a result, organizations often find that they still face a variety of unresolved concerns.

Since information technology initiatives tend to involve sizable investments of money and resources, responsible managers will usually not agree to go ahead with implementation plans until they have some means of identifying potential problems. Testing the proposed solution in the field is likely the best way to accomplish this, especially if nonstandard technology is involved, or if the plans call for sweeping changes to the organization. In such situations, extra time and a limited-risk methodology such as an application pilot should be seriously considered. Organizations should avoid making substantial investments in a fully operational system until they have hard data about its probable effects.

This chapter starts by examining the reasons for choosing to run an application pilot, then goes on to discuss the types of pilots you might consider and how to organize and analyse them. The intent is to help you address the issues involved in the development and implementation of an effective application pilot.

#  RATIONALE FOR APPLICATION PILOTS

A pilot design methodology is best based on a strategy for determining customized systems solutions — that is, solutions based on the specific requirements of your organization and personnel. An application pilot provides a safe testing ground for working through areas of concern or uncertainty in your LAN implementation. Undertaking a pilot project provides these benefits:

- Learning the specifics of how a system will affect the organization, before implementation

- Reducing those ever-present "grey areas" in solution design and implementation planning

- Obtaining an initial low-risk exposure to the problems of managing organizational change

- Preparing the users for change

- Providing training in the use of the technology

- Acquiring data on the benefits of the system and on the users' adaptation to it, through experience

- Building the new system's visibility

Probably the sole disadvantage of application pilots is that they do add time and sometimes costs to a LAN implementation.

However simple or complex a pilot project may be, it is important that a plan be established and formally approved before the pilot officially starts. The plan for an application pilot should include the following:

CHECK
LIST

✔ Project objectives and methodology

✔ Criteria for evaluation and success

✔ A **detailed pilot specification document** similar to the functional requirements specification document

✔ A statement of work which lists milestones, deliverables, target dates, and accountabilities

✔ A detailed project schedule

✔ Budget guidelines

While each piece of this plan is important, it is critical that the detailed pilot specification document be based on information drawn from the functional requirements specification document. The decision to undertake an application pilot should, as mentioned above, result from the desire to resolve some apparent problem in the proposed system solution design. Any problem area will be identified in the functional requirements specification document. We have too often seen organizations attempt to short-circuit the planning process by drafting a pilot specification from a certain application that they want to see implemented. This may get the particular application up and running, but does little for its integration with the system as a whole.

The detailed pilot specification document provides the implementation project team with the following information:

CHECK
LIST

✔ A description of the pilot system's features and functionality, which may simply be a subset of the functionality laid out in the functional requirements specification document

✔ A description of how the pilot system will mesh with the pilot user environment

✔ Most of the information needed for purchasing the appropriate pilot hardware and software

✔ A technical design specification for the design, installation, and set-up of the pilot system

Like any component of the STEPS process, your application pilot plan should include a series of observation checkpoints at which findings and recommendations are reported to management. It is the pilot project leader's duty to keep the relevant managers posted throughout the pilot so they will encounter no surprises. The managers are to be given the opportunity to comment and suggest changes as they see fit. Taking this approach reduces the margin of error and enhances the managers' confidence and acceptance, since they feel that it is their project and that they contributed to its outcome.

# TYPES OF APPLICATION PILOTS

Since application pilots vary in complexity, many different types of pilot systems exist. The typical examples to be considered here are the small pilot group, the single application pilot, the incremental pilot, and the live operational data pilot. Each is discussed in turn below.

## Small Pilot Group

A small pilot group is usually composed of between 20 and 50 select people. The scope of such a pilot varies with each project, generally involving several distinct or integrated applications. The effects of the pilot are assessed by the comparison of control groups.

In this type of pilot, the untested technology application is handled in one of two ways. The first approach gives the members of the group a subset of the proposed operational applications, that is, some working examples. For instance, the end users might be offered a package of electronic mail, word processing, accounting, and presentation capabilities.

The second method involves offering a superset of new applications. In this case, the test group is given a large number of applications, and the implementors have the opportunity to observe the group members selecting the most appropriate system features and applications. For example, the users might be offered electronic mail and direct file-to-fax capabilities, as well as several word processing, accounting, and presentation packages. This approach is inviting to consider, since it tends to lead to more interesting results. Nonetheless, you should be aware that successful "natural selection" by the users depends greatly on their level of computer literacy and/or the user friendliness of the applications.

## Single Application Pilot

This type of pilot involves the deployment of one particular application within a select group of users. For instance, groupware software such as Microsoft Office may be implemented within a select work group. After the system effects are evaluated, the scope of the pilot may be extended with regard to numbers of user groups and/or functionality. The advantage of the single application pilot lies in both its simplicity and the control it offers. Its disadvantage, compared to the small group pilot, is that it is limited to a single application.

## Incremental Pilot

In an incremental pilot, new hardware and software are added to an existing information system. For example, a new financial application such as Payroll may be integrated with an accounting system which has been in use for several years. The advantages of the incremental pilot are that it vastly simplifies start-up, training, and logistics, and that it allows costs to be more readily controlled. In essence, you are dealing with fewer unknowns. This type of pilot is generally used when an organization is considering making some adjustments to an existing system, rather than completely overhauling it.

## Live Operational Data Pilot

As the name suggests, this pilot is based on live operational information such as a database. For example, the existing main database may be enhanced with changes or additional features and capabilities, including new inquiry or data entry screens, the generation of new reports, and the like. The advantage of the live operational data pilot is that it allows you to verify that the new capabilities do, in fact, provide the desired solution, before you abandon the original methodology. Its main drawback is that critical live information forms the core of the pilot. Therefore, extra precautions must be taken to avoid data failures and problems with data integrity.

## ORGANIZING AND ANALYSING THE APPLICATION PILOT

The application pilot is normally developed and run by the implementation project team. Ultimate responsibility for it rests with the project leader. However, the actual work on the pilot project is often delegated to the technology advisor, who in this capacity is sometimes referred to as the pilot project leader (as on page 52). For the sake of clarity, the title used throughout this book will be technology advisor.

The application pilot may be thought of as occurring in three stages: the pre-pilot stage, the pilot stage, and the operational stage. At the conclusion of each, a presentation is made to management to ensure ongoing contact, understanding, and support for the pilot project. At the pre-pilot stage, the LAN implementation project leader may work with the technology advisor on the management presentation. Once the pilot is underway, the technology advisor usually handles all such presentations and is also responsible for consolidating the pilot results with comments from management in an **application pilot summary report**. The information in the report is then fed back into the design and development of the implementation by the technology advisor.

## Pre-Pilot Stage

At this preliminary stage comes the development of precise specifications, evaluation criteria, project schedules, and budgets, in conjunction with a series of investigations similar to those used to draw up the functional requirements specification document. All these items are necessary for preparing the application pilot plan.

Initially, the appropriate managers are briefed on key aspects of the pilot project, its methodology, and the make-up of the pilot project team. The technology advisor reviews related organizational documentation, organizational charts, planning documents, and corporate objective statements. He or she also holds interviews to gain a better understanding of the following aspects of the proposed pilot group environment:

- Organizational objectives for the pilot

- Suggested areas of improvement, such as increased efficiency

- Current use of information technology

- The pilot group's past history and experiences

In addition, the technology advisor should issue a questionnaire to a sampling of key end users. This survey is somewhat more specific than the functional requirements specification outline and is designed to elicit information about the users' expectations of improved effectiveness —

what they will be able to do and how. The questionnaire investigates current practices, business needs, attitudes, opportunities, and risks. If designed appropriately, this pre-implementation material may be useful for the following purposes:

- Developing evaluation criteria for pre-test and post-test review of the effects of the new technology

- Helping in the customization of the pilot analysis criteria and various systems of measurement

- Familiarizing management with the pilot project

- Giving the technology advisor both a clearer view of the organization and the information required for writing up the detailed pilot specification document

Once these preliminaries have been completed, the technology advisor can develop the application pilot plan for presentation. Finally, he or she obtains approval for the work plan, deliverables, and costs.

## Pilot Stage

The pilot team commences this stage by using the approved detailed pilot specification document as the blueprint by which to construct the pilot system. The application pilot is then implemented according to the agreed-upon statement of work and project schedule.

Throughout the pilot stage, the use of the system is monitored in an automated fashion. The end users' responses are obtained and measured in accordance with pilot-specific criteria, by means of structured interviews, observation of training sessions, logs, and unobtrusive observation of system use. A cycle of sampling and feedback is used to continually adjust and refine the pilot system. The refinements can range from simple fine-tuning and debugging to substantial application design modifications.

At the conclusion of the pilot stage, the technology advisor presents the findings and recommendations to management. Then, after obtaining approval for the recommendations, he or she consolidates all the material into a preliminary summary report.

# Operational Stage

Once the pilot has been successfully implemented for the period established in the project schedule, the pilot project team has access to various measured results regarding the effectiveness of the applications. If appropriate, this information forms the basis for the extension of the pilot into the final operational system. The data also let the technology advisor extrapolate the effects of a fully operational system with some confidence, as well as develop a reasonably accurate picture of associated costs and benefits.

At this stage, the pilot project team presents the relevant managers with the application pilot summary report, which summarizes the main findings and recommendations, in order to persuade them of the feasibility of the system. The report focuses on the following four areas of the project: system monitoring, post-pilot testing, rationale and recommendations, and cost justification. Each of these is discussed below.

## System Monitoring

Available usage statistics generated by the system are summarized, to give a picture of system use. Included are the use of various applications, resource utilization, and so on.

## Post-pilot Testing

The instruments from the original pilot systems analysis are re-administered to both the pilot group and any control groups. This is done in order to evaluate the effects of the system, and to compare anticipated effects with actual effects. It is here that the material from the questionnaires issued at the pre-pilot stage comes into play.

## Rationale and Recommendations

Any recommendation that calls for changes to the functional requirements specification document should be highlighted and accompanied by a rationale. This is a vital part of the operational stage of the application pilot, since it relates the pilot results directly to the proposed system solution report and thereby allows a better customized design to be developed for your organization's LAN.

Once management has approved the application pilot summary report, the technology advisor updates both the functional requirements specification document and the system solution report to reflect the recommendations in the pilot summary. It is generally true that the application pilot will have been undertaken to help justify the introduction of a LAN, and to test for any unknowns relating to it. Therefore, the recommendations in the application pilot summary report will help the project team convince management to let the implementation move on to Phase II of the STEPS process, installation preparation.

## Cost Justification

To develop an effective cost justification, the effects of the pilot system must be considered together with all recommended changes to the proposed system solution. These points are derived from pilot system monitoring and post-pilot testing. Taken together, they create the cost-benefit analysis of your application pilot. (The components of a cost-benefit analysis are detailed in Chapter 5.)

Once the cost-benefit analysis has been presented to management and approved, the project team may continue with the LAN implementation.

• • • • • • • • • • • • •
COST-BENEFIT ANALYSIS

· · · · · · · · · · · · · · · · · ·

## COST-BENEFIT ANALYSIS

It has already been pointed out that information technology almost always involves substantial investments of money and resources. Consequently, most organizations wish to examine carefully the costs versus the anticipated benefits before moving ahead with any proposed solution. This examination is known as a **cost-benefit analysis** or **business case**.

A business case is most successful when it is based on the overall effect of the technology on your organization. That is, to be effective, it must be related not only to organizational performance — overall corporate objectives — but also to improvements in operational efficiency.

Certain steps should always be included in a cost-benefit analysis. However, it must be kept in mind that the key issues in the analysis should be linked to the specific goals of your organization. This chapter discusses the basics of developing cost-benefit analyses, and also considers some current organizational trends that may affect the way in which you assess cost-benefits.

## TIMING A COST-BENEFIT ANALYSIS

A cost-benefit analysis is normally developed as part of any proposed technology solution and is adequate for addressing the costing issues of a proposed implementation. On occasion, however, there may be unresolved concerns about a recommended solution, so you may have to develop a more precise business case to win management approval.

In such a situation, an application pilot is undertaken before the cost-benefit analysis is developed. This sequence provides a realistic evaluation of the benefits, opportunities, and risks associated with the project. The application pilot lets your organization work with the recommended technology, minimize related expenditures and operating difficulties, and at the same time acquire data on its costs and effectiveness. Once the pilot project is completed, a far more convincing business case can be argued — one that is based on actual experience related to both organizational performance and operational efficiency benefits.

# ORGANIZATIONAL PERFORMANCE

The criteria selected for measuring organizational performance should be directly linked to your organization's corporate objectives. While objectives vary from firm to firm, they are fairly easy to quantify. Common performance-measuring criteria include the following:

- Generation of revenue

- Profitability

- Market share

- Product quality and returns

- Return on investment (ROI)

# OPERATIONAL EFFICIENCY

Operational efficiency measures, on the other hand, are directly related to your organization's operational costs and the effectiveness of internal resources. They may or may not be easy to quantify. Criteria for measuring operational efficiency include these:

- Reduction in costs (e.g., for rented floor space, telephone bills, etc.)

- Quantification of time savings

- Reduction in labour activities (e.g., procedural streamlining to free staff for more useful activity)

The only reasonable basis for quantifying operational efficiency and productivity benefits is the combination of hard dollar, soft dollar, and qualitative benefits. Each of these is discussed separately below.

## Hard Dollar Benefits

Hard dollar benefits result in quantifiable, direct financial savings. The following are some areas where such cost reductions may be realized:

- Office space

- Administrative overhead

- Employee overtime

- Travel

- Telecommunications

- Number of employees

## Soft Dollar Benefits

Soft dollar benefits are measurable savings or improvements which can be translated into meaningful dollar values, but which may not be, in themselves, direct financial savings. Here are some examples of this category of benefits:

- Reduction in the time required for setting up meetings or connecting successfully with individuals by telephone

- Reduction of managerial activities, as a result of delegation to subordinates

- Reduction of business time spent in travel

- Reduction of support requirements resulting from managerial use of automated tools which frees staff to do other tasks

## Qualitative Benefits

Qualitative benefits are those which may be measurable, but which do not easily lend themselves to dollar equivalencies. Examples include the following:

• Reduction in daily interruptions, leading to greater productivity

• Improvement in morale

• Faster turnaround

# PRESENTING A COST-BENEFIT ANALYSIS

It is usual practice for management to offer support for an investment — particularly a costly one — only after its value and implications are fully understood. As stated above, the primary purpose of a cost-benefit analysis is to persuade management of the feasibility of a proposal. Any number of methods may be used to accomplish this goal. More important than the approach is the ability to evaluate the issues clearly and present concise business arguments.

A successful cost-benefit analysis therefore begins with the education of your organization's management. This is not such a difficult task, since the business case usually follows the needs analysis and/or the application pilot, which have already afforded the opportunity to involve management in the process. Hence there is little or no element of surprise when management is offered an assessment of anticipated changes to corporate objectives for a specific user group, arising from the implementation. This assessment, which is usually based on the pilot project data collected, ideally is applicable throughout the organization. Management is also offered an assessment of projected operational efficiency benefits, which are typically broken down into the three categories discussed earlier: hard dollar, soft dollar, and qualitative benefits. The aim of the entire exercise is to help management identify and relate to the tangible benefits associated with the venture. Distinguishing between hard dollar and soft dollar benefits is particularly helpful in this regard.

The presentation of a business case usually covers effects on performance, efficiency benefits, and time savings items. It invariably includes a detailed financial analysis. An example is provided by a law firm with which we have worked. Wishing to provide better service and reduce overhead costs, the firm chose to enhance an existing LAN, adding a number of automated presentation tools and expanding direct access to the electronic message system and document pool. The cost-benefit presentation examined the enhancement items and how they improved the firm's work. For example, documents were developed and revised faster; supporting and presentation material was easier to produce; less time that could be billed for was expended on tasks with low financial return; and so on. These efficiencies were then translated into overall corporate goals — to cut costs and become more responsive — and presented as effects on performance. Any financial statement that accompanied the cost-benefit analysis could indicate higher profitability because of the reductions in overhead.

The time savings benefits on which a cost-benefit analysis is partly based may be difficult to assess. If this is the case, then it is wise to include a time re-investment strategy that describes how to make use of such opportunities. Organization structure, employees' tasks, or certain procedures may need to be reviewed and changed, to take advantage of time savings. Consider, once again, the law firm discussed above. When the firm's enhancement of its LAN expanded direct access to the electronic message system and document pool, all the lawyers gained direct access to the firm's documents and were able to handle their own in-house written messages. Over several months of recorded observation, the firm determined that the majority of the lawyers derived three inter-related benefits from the change. First, the legal assistant who used to handle all correspondence and the sourcing of documents was freed from these tasks and had more time available for undertaking other work. Second, the lawyers found that they were getting responses to their messages more rapidly, since the support staff had more time to devote to support functions such as those required for providing faster responses to inquiries. The lawyers also found that, even though they were now handling their own messages, they actually spent less time dictating to and directing the support staff. This freed the lawyers for other tasks, such as meeting with clients. The re-investment strategy for this firm would examine where both the assistants' and the lawyers' new-found free time would best be spent. For instance, the firm might choose to continue on its present path, simply dealing with its current workload in a more cost-effective way. A more common approach today would be for the firm to undertake a new initiative with the extra time its existing resources have available.

## Financial Analysis

Both hard dollar and soft dollar benefits are factored into the cost-benefit analysis. However, most organizations need to see hard dollar benefits to adopt any proposed plan for new technology. All hard dollar savings must be represented with associated costs in the financial analysis section of the business case. This section should provide at least a two-year view, broken down by quarter. It normally includes a spreadsheet printout, showing a contribution analysis or return on investment, together with all assumptions that were built into the analysis.

# ORGANIZATIONAL TRENDS

In assessing the effects of a new technology strategy, it is important to be aware of general organizational trends. These were discussed in Chapter 1 and are briefly restated here, because we believe that they constitute a fundamental re-evaluation of where real organizational or operational benefits are to be found. They offer a new perspective on soft dollar benefits which at another time may not have been seriously considered and which may cause you to rethink how you weight the value of all soft dollar benefits in a cost-benefit analysis.

Organizations today understand that, in order to achieve their corporate goals and remain competitive, all their business units must be responsive and flexible. With respect to information technology — including LANs — responsiveness and flexibility often call for some corporate restructuring, as well as the decentralization and distribution of specific information application functions. Senior managers are aware that front-line personnel need additional skills and improved automated information tools.

These trends suggest a changed view of how business is done, and for what purpose information systems — both mainframe and LAN — are used. Of utmost concern for senior management is accountability, given the transfer of control to smaller, distributed business units. Managers also recognize the need to alter current management processes and procedures. This goal may be attained by introducing co-ordinated and distributed planning to safeguard corporate standards and eliminate the duplication of resources and services. Yet another concern for management stems from the existing level of technical skills within the organization's business units. Workers typically need sound training and development programs. In addition, it may be necessary to relocate some key information technology staff among the units to speed the transfer of technical knowledge to the front line. Finally, today's managers recognize the need for improved data management, which improves co-ordination and integration among all business units.

************************

In conclusion, the success of your cost-benefit analysis is directly dependent on your organization's ability to assess its hard dollar benefits and to come to terms with new soft dollar benefits, such as those resulting from the rethinking of organizational roles and responsibilities.

STRATEGIC OPERATIONAL
PLANS

# CHAPTER 6

# STRATEGIC OPERATIONAL PLANS

Central to any successful LAN implementation is the ability to develop not only the technical design of the system but also the plans required for supporting the effective, secure operation of the network. This chapter presents a range of issues that your organization must consider before approving any proposed technology solution. As you read through it, keep in mind that the chapter offers only a guideline. Its intent is to make you aware of certain elements of strategic operational planning which are all too often overlooked, especially in small to mid-sized organizations. The following strategic operational plans are discussed in this chapter:

- Security plan

- Back-up plan

- Disaster recovery plan

- Support plan

- System acceptance test plan

- Training plan

- Financial plan

One of the advantages of using the STEPS process is that it remains constant regardless of organizational goals or the details of a given LAN implementation. On the other hand, all good strategic operational plans must be tailored to reflect these details. Every organization will, of necessity, have a different set of operational requirements for LAN implementation, arising from the solution chosen and the work environment.

Your completed strategic operational plans will be a blueprint for staff operations relating to security, back-up, disaster recovery, support, system acceptance, and training. They will also include a financial analysis detailing the budgetary costs involved in implementing the solution. These plans are undertaken during Phase I of the STEPS process, and are primarily the responsibility of the technology advisor. They are based on the information about your organization contained in the needs analysis study and the site inspection report. When complete, the strategic operational plans form essential components of the approved system solution report.

We would like to be able to provide a complete template for the development of each of the strategic operational plans; however, their specialized nature and complexity make this impossible. If your project team requires a greater level of detail, you may be wise to arrange for the participation of an outside party with the experience needed for your implementation.

The rest of the chapter will examine the strategic operational plans listed above, in as much detail as feasible.

# S ECURITY PLAN

The security plan is a vital component of any LAN implementation. It provides both the information security methodology and the related set-up instructions, as well as a set of evaluation criteria for measuring its own success.

The existence of a network virtually presupposes significant problems concerning information access, control, and security. Users want to be able to access all information, at any time, anywhere. On the other hand, computer viruses are multiplying at an alarming rate. The LAN administrator therefore walks a fine line between too much and too little security. Too little protection leaves the LAN vulnerable to intrusion; too much is regarded as intrusive by the users, who will seek ways to bypass security measures.

There are two main approaches to securing protection in the LAN environment. The first and more common is the use of adminstrative software (found within the network operating system) for establishing resource access rights and privileges. It requires a thorough understanding of the chosen network operating system, the standalone and network applications, and the users and common interest groups and their various resource-sharing needs. The second way of protecting a network relies on special security products, such as data encryption devices.

If your organization has an existing information security plan, it should be used as a basis for developing the LAN security plan. If, however, your information security plan does not appear relevant or adaptable, it should be updated to accommodate the implementation. In either case, the project team, your corporate information group, and a third party with expertise in this area should collaborate on the work.

## The Security Audit

In developing a LAN security plan, the first task is to perform a three-stage security audit. You begin by assessing all risks and exposures. Then you consider the end users, including their needs, skill sets, and environment, and whether any of them belongs to a high-risk group. Lastly, you evaluate the management and supervisory structures within your organization and on your network. Each of these factors is examined below.

### Risks and Exposures

In the context of LAN security, **risk** refers to the possibility of loss, theft, or corruption of the information on the network. **Exposure** is rather more complex. One element of exposure is how capable you are of determining who requires access to what information. Another is how easy it is to access the network from the outside; here, "outside" can refer to someone from another work unit within the organization, or to an intruder from outside the organization. A third aspect of exposure is your ability to trace an intrusion and block further occurrences.

When analyzing risks and exposures, you focus on how much you can afford to lose and how likely you are to lose it. You need to determine the nature of information that is or will be stored on the network, the nature of information that may not be stored on the network, and the ease with which all this information can be accessed. There are two basic issues to be addressed:

- Who is the rightful owner of the information?

- Who else requires direct access to the information?

The answers are discovered through the development of the needs analysis study and the site inspection report. You will find more information about this in Chapter 8.

The basis for establishing access is this question: Why does the user need direct access, and is the need legitimate? The principle that governs the answer is the **need-to-know rule**: A user should have access only to the information that he or she actually requires. This rule applies to virtually all corporate information, some of which may be considered sensitive, some not. It is wise to safeguard even information which is not considered sensitive, if only to avoid the inconvenience of its loss or corruption.

The security audit identifies the individuals who need to know the information on your network and defines them by work group and job function in the security plan. Just as end user profile worksheets profile the users, directory planning worksheets and security profile worksheets can be used to map out directories and access requirements. Both these types of worksheets will be illustrated and discussed in depth in Chapter 8.

## Users

The second factor in the security audit is the users themselves and the way they are organized. If your organization is comprised of work groups, your access decisions will be simpler. If not, think about the users in terms of the functions they perform and their common computing requirements, then categorize them into departments — accounts payable, product marketing, and so forth. When workers such as managers cross departmental lines, they should be considered part of their own work group for control purposes. Suppose, for example, that Peter Holland, VP Finance, heads up the accounting department but requires access to a product marketing database so he can forecast revenues. Holland should be treated as part of the accounting group. This is a more manageable approach in large, complex organizations than creating additional work groups consisting of users who need to share information.

Grouping users on the basis of job function and computing requirements allows you to contain damage to critical data, whether caused accidentally or intentionally. Since it lets you identify legitimate users and trace their actions, it also helps in tracing users' errors and intrusions.

Some groups are, by definition, high-risk users. They require access to very sensitive information or have wide-ranging access capabilities, such as dial-up modems. These users should be pinpointed and their requirements closely evaluated. In certain instances, you may elect to move them onto their own area of the system to minimize exposure. Traditionally, high-risk groups are the finance and personnel departments. In today's environment, computer-literate senior executives and individuals or work groups that deal on-line with outside data sources are also high-risk.

## Management and Supervisors

One common fallacy in the development of security planning is the belief that department heads should have global access to the network just because they are the bosses. In fact, managers should not be granted these privileges unless they require specific information in order to perform their jobs. Another fallacy is that the LAN administrator should be given full responsibility for global network security. Again, this should not be the case unless your organization or LAN operation is quite small.

In managing security, a technique known as compartmentalization is commonly used. It is not dissimilar to the categorization of the users into departments, as discussed above. Compartmentalization conforms to the need-to-know rule, and dictates that as few people as possible should have full knowledge of the entire operation. No-one should know any more than what is essential for performing his or her assigned task.

In the allocation of security among the network management staff, network supervisors generally need the broadest access to the network, usually for reasons of support. LAN administrators are usually responsible for one network segment or work group. Security officers have to be able to see and audit the entire network, but without necessarily being able to change anything without a supervisor's assistance. Every system should have a security plan and security officer. In smaller environments, it is tempting to combine the roles of network supervisor and security officer. We have seen examples where all security duties were handled by one individual. Nevertheless, it is wise to take advantage of the checks and balances associated with having at least two people filling the positions of network supervisor, LAN administrator, and security officer. Another benefit is that the organization faces less difficulty when one of these people quits or retires.

## Developing a Security Plan

Once the security audit has been completed, you are ready to develop the security plan itself. When doing so, it is important to remain mindful of the five main elements of security:

- Authorization: You need to authorize users, actions, and resources.

- Identification: Users, groups, devices, programs, and transactions must be identified.

- Access control: You must control access to the system, actions on system resources, and information elements such as database records.

- Accountability: You have to account for users, actions, and resources, usually by means of a detailed system log that provides an audit through reports and monitoring.

- Auditability: Your system log must allow for reconstruction of pre-disaster data and the reasons for any disaster.

To sort out and present security needs in an organized way, you could use a structured format which examines the following topics: access levels and definitions; work groups; rules governing access; physical installation and access security guidelines; internetwork connections; levels of administration and accountability; security audit policy; and software. These eight points represent the minimum amount of information that should be included in your completed security plan. Each point is examined in turn below.

### Access Levels and Definitions

This section of the security plan specifically defines all access levels; for instance, 01 = Top Priority, Global Access.

### Work Groups

This section of the security plan names all user groups, and specifies how each fits into the LAN's access rules. For example, the finance department is one work group; it has global access to all accounting applications and restricts access to such information by other users on a group-by-group basis. Product marketing is another department; it has limited access to accounting applications and partial access to sales reporting and inventory control.

### Rules Governing Access

This section contains a statement outlining access rules, such as password policy and volume access.

### Physical Installation and Access Security Guidelines

This part of the security plan details the physical installation and access security guidelines, and covers the addition of special security protection equipment such as data encryption devices.

### Internetwork Connections

All internetwork connections and their security access requirements are itemized here.

### Levels of Administration and Accountability

This section clearly and specifically sets out who is responsible for what.

### Security Audit Policy

This section indicates how and when the security plan is to be reviewed.

### Software

This section lists all software. It also provides details of the upgrade, auditing, installation, and software license auditing policies.

**************************

Once the LAN security plan has been developed, it must be included in the system solution report. It must also be approved by senior management and made part of corporate policy. A corporate system security officer administers the plan, which should be reviewed annually, if not more often.

## Administrative Guidelines for LAN Security

The LAN security plan must contain the tools for providing evidence of intrusion, locating and identifying any intruder, containing damage, and restoring corrupted data. If you fail to implement the guidelines in the plan, you will not have a secure system. The users and administrators are also essential in ensuring that the security plan works.

You start securing your LAN by using all the network administration tools for compartmentalizing users and information. Access control and user privileges can be at the level of individual volumes and directories, or even individual files if the LAN operating system allows. Carry the need-to-know rule as far as you can within the limits of your system's inherent security capabilities.

Next you define the users and the information to which they require access. Their access requirements are documented in the security plan. By stating who can go where in the network and what they can do when they get there, you will have met a large portion of your security needs.

You should also establish a level of access control which requires users to identify themselves, but which does not inconvenience them to the extent that they will attempt to bypass security. Typically, if users feel that the existing security measures cause them undue difficulty in doing  their jobs, they try to circumvent those measures. They may, for instance, move their work off the network, which defeats virtually all the reasons for introducing the LAN and greatly endangers the security of their data.

## A Closer Look at Access Control

The concept of "access" keeps cropping up in this chapter. Access control is the first line of defence against users who are not permitted to see or use network resources. As such, it is worth a closer look.

Proper access control requires all users to be identified as valid on the network, authorized for the type of access required, and verified as to whether they are who they claim to be. These three requirements can be met in a number of ways. The stringency with which this is done is proportional to the sensitivity of the information.

Networks are secured from the outside in. Access control must therefore operate at each gateway to information: the workstation, directory, file, record, internetwork, and so on. As mentioned, there are various methods of providing access control, some internal to the network and its operating system, others external.

At the workstation, the first level of access control, a common approach is to use a network password for assigning a combination of user privileges and resource rights. In more sensitive systems, an additional layer of security may be established with a second-level password or a token (smart card) device.

The disk drives are the next level of concern. Data on the network disk drives must be protected. If an unauthorized party accesses your network, the door to your corporate information is open via the disk drives. Encryption guarantees that only legitimate users and applications have access to the contents of your files.

Each network segment is a gateway to data. However, security between segments is often difficult to establish because of the assumption that users on one part of the system should have access to any other part. This is no more true for this level than for the individual workstation application. Protection of network segments may be as simple as checking user IDs and passwords. Amazingly, many sensitive systems are "protected" at this level by a user named Tech who has the password Support. Intruders usually know such common user IDs and passwords as these, or Guest or User.

Whenever data leave one LAN to travel to another LAN, a mainframe, or an internetwork, interception over the wire may be a concern. All such data should be considered for encryption. Several systems allow information to be encrypted as it travels along the wire.

No access control measure, however sophisticated, is worth anything if legitimate users do not protect their means of access. They must understand and value their ability to manage passwords, tokens, and/or personal identification numbers (PINs), in order to prevent their misuse. Access control begins with the system but relies on the users for its success.

*************************

Securing your LAN calls for a combination of common sense and co-operation on the part of the users, the full use of the administrative safeguards built into network operating systems, and, if your risk/exposure assessment so indicates, the addition of external devices for extra protection.

# B ACK-UP PLAN

The purpose of developing a back-up plan is to create an organized, documented method for avoiding the loss or corruption of information. This strategic operational plan is designed to ensure that all data are copied on a regular basis and exist in duplicate. It thereby protects your organization in the event that your security plan fails and a virus enters your system; or the firm is exposed to some catastrophe, such as a fire; or a worker inadvertently erases some vital information.

Every back-up plan should combine safety considerations — for the protection of data — and convenience — for the benefit of the users and/or clients. The latter aspect is essential, because, if the plan is difficult to follow, then those responsible for performing back-ups will find ways to avoid doing so.

Your back-up plan should cover the following matters:

- A summary of LAN site information back-up needs, detailing what needs to be backed up — volumes, directories, file lists, etc. — and when

- A description of the back-up systems to be used, such as tape, disk-to-disk, and so on

- Recycle methods for the back-up media, for example, monthly recycling of daily tapes

- The details of how to back up the information — for example, manually or automatically — and the procedures involved, such as back-up log maintenance

- Storage facilities for all back-up media, on or off site

- Restore procedures, which explain how to retrieve any lost or corrupted information

Since back-ups are essentially periodic, the plan is usually presented in terms of the back-up cycles: daily, weekly, monthly, quarterly, and annual. The plan establishes the time of day, the media to be used, and who is responsible for doing back-ups. For example, your business may require a daily back-up of all data on tape, to be performed by the LAN administrator at 5:00 p.m. In large environments with several LAN administrators, each is responsible for backing up his or her own work group's information. The back-up plan and the accompanying back-up log serve as a documentation aid for the LAN administrator(s) during full system operation.

Servers often come equipped with tape back-up systems. A commonly used tape back-up strategy employs three separate sets of daily back-ups, each done in successive weeks. In the fourth week, the tapes from the first set are re-used; two sets of complete back-ups are still available in case something goes wrong during the fourth back-up. In the fifth week, the tapes from the second set are re-used. This approach offers the security of two earlier sets of back-ups in addition to the current one.

It is important to note that many back-up systems employ an automatic scheduler. The back-up schedule is pre-programmed into the system, which performs an unattended back-up at the appropriate time. This feature is very useful when large quantities of data are to be backed up after normal business hours.

## Types of Back-ups

There are two main categories of back-ups: full and incremental. In a **full back-up**, you effectively save all your selected files at once. Restoring the information involves simply loading your last full back-up and selecting the files you wish to restore. You may restore the entire disk, if necessary. A full back-up is the simplest and safest way to make certain that all your files are backed up and can easily be restored.

In an **incremental back-up**, only those files which have been created, copied, or modified since the last back-up — whether full or incremental — are saved. Since most files do not change from one back-up to the next, incremental back-ups can be a good interim solution that saves on time and media. Unfortunately, restoring your information from an incremental back-up is more complicated and prone to error than doing so from a full back-up, because you must often restore the last full back-up, then all subsequent incremental back-ups.

A possible approach is to combine the two types of back-ups by doing daily incremental back-ups between weekly and monthly full back-ups. Typically, large organizations use only full back-ups, because of the ease and speed with which restoration can take place. For the same reasons, we recommend the use of full back-ups for smaller organizations as well.

## The Back-up Log

The back-up log (Figure 6.1) provides ongoing documentation of back-up procedures. It must always be both current and accurate. If it is not, then data restoration will be difficult, and your organization's disaster recovery plan, which includes the back-up plan, will be adversely affected.

# Back-up Log

Ref ID: BL - 930101000

Server ID:  ServerX

Location:  2B1

Server Function:  Accounting Files

*Audit Trail*

| Tape ID | Date/Time | Back-up Type (Full/Incremental) | Backed Up By | Notes |
|---------|-----------|--------------------------------|--------------|-------|
| 93D0001 | 93/01/21 | Full | M. Miller | Daily Back-up |
| 93D0002 | 93/01/22 | Full | M. Miller | Daily Back-up |
| 93D0003 | 93/01/25 | Full | M. Miller | Daily Back-up |
| 93D0004 | 93/01/26 | Full | M. Rubin | Daily Back-up |
| 93D0005 | 93/01/27 | Full | M. Rubin | Daily Back-up |
| 93D0006 | 93/01/28 | Full | M. Rubin | Daily Back-up |
| 93D0007 | 93/01/29 | Full | M. Rubin | Daily Back-up |
| 93M0001 | 93/01/31 | Full | J. Franco | Monthly Back-up |
| 93D0001 | 93/02/01 | Full | J.Franco | Daily Back-up |
|  |  |  |  |  |
|  |  |  |  |  |
|  |  |  |  |  |
|  |  |  |  |  |
|  |  |  |  |  |
|  |  |  |  |  |
|  |  |  |  |  |
|  |  |  |  |  |
|  |  |  |  |  |
|  |  |  |  |  |

*Figure 6.1: Back-up Log*

The back-up log represents your organization's dated record of the following:

- Who is performing the back-up

- What medium (disk, tape, or other) is being used

- Whether the back-up is full or incremental

# DISASTER RECOVERY PLAN

The disaster recovery plan is designed to protect against network-related catastrophic failures beyond the organization's control, and possibly originating from outside the building. It should encompass both voice and data networks.

With the growth of LANs and the distribution of departmental functions to front-line work units, a great deal of critical information is being stored. Most organizations fail to devote sufficient thought to protection plans for the data. When information is moved from a mainframe to a LAN, the local user or administrator is responsible for its safety. This individual may well be unaware of the dangers inherent in leaving an unprotected LAN in operation.

Every organization should have a disaster protection plan, regardless of the size of the network. Determining how much protection is appropriate can be difficult, however, and can affect both the structure and the cost of facilities within and outside of the LAN site complex. Overprotection is needlessly expensive, while underprotection can leave the network vulnerable.

Fortunately, you have many choices when determining the type and scope of a disaster protection plan, including these:

- Uninterruptable power supplies

- Off-site storage of back-up media

- Multiple entry points to the building, multiple trunk routes from the common carrier central office, and multiple central offices

- An alternate recovery location for use in the event of a major disaster such as a fire, complete with compatible computing equipment and telecommunications facilities, as well as a crisis management team and vendor support

## Developing a Disaster Recovery Plan

The first stage is to determine your organization's level of risk. This investigation is best handled by a vendor, consulting firm, or other third party with experience in these matters. You should select a firm which has conducted audits on businesses of all sizes, and which should therefore be capable of determining whether your organization is operating at an unacceptable level of risk. Your project team's involvement here will depend on the members' own capabilities in this area and the outside resources available. Its principal role will be to make sure that the disaster recovery plan developed does, in fact, meet the needs of your particular system.

Once risk level has been established, your choices for a contingency plan depend primarily on how quickly you must be back in business. The following issues, which are often set out in the corporate information technology plan, must also be addressed:

- What type of disaster do you wish to plan for — fire, flooding, earthquake, loss of telephone company central office, etc.?

- What are your key business functions, and which computing systems are needed to support them?

- What is the deadline by which you must recover and have these applications back in operation?

The disaster recovery plan outlines the disaster recovery methodology chosen, the alternate recovery location(s), and key contacts and telephone numbers that may be required. It also provides instructions on reporting to the recovery location(s), organizing the crisis management team and starting the recovery process (that is, retrieving stored data and using the standby recovery system, and effectively using vendors to expedite delivery of essential hardware and software). Finally, it lists the organization's business functions by priority. Critical functions should be highlighted and their supporting computer systems noted, together with security and access information.

Once the plan has been completed, the project team should test it to make certain that it works as intended. If it does, the disaster recovery plan is ready for inclusion in the system solution report. The plan should be tested at least once a year, and updated to reflect changes in your organization.

At least one copy of the disaster recovery plan should be stored at the alternate recovery location where your crisis management team will meet to conduct the recovery process. If this disaster recovery facility is at a different location than the restore site, another copy should be kept with the standby recovery system. Yet another copy should be kept at the off-site storage facility where the main back-up is found. Each member of the crisis management team should also have a copy.

A sound disaster recovery plan is good insurance. Without it, your best hope is to retrieve your hard drive and attempt to restore your data. Like all strategic operational plans, the disaster recovery plan should be a dynamic, up-to-date document.

# **S** UPPORT PLAN

The support plan is intended to give the organization a structured approach to providing technical or applications support for each group of end users. It is also designed to identify, track, and resolve applications-related and technical problems.

To accomplish these goals, you must devise a support plan which reflects organizational objectives, user needs, and available resources. The plan should set out a clear problem escalation process which describes methods for dealing with various levels of difficulties — in brief, whom to call and when — together with procedures for documenting all resultant changes in the **network maintenance logs**. An example of a network maintenance log — an essential component of a successful implementation — may be seen in Figure 6.2.

If your support plan fails to meet these requirements and problems arise in your implementation, then your support resources will likely appear ineffective and disorganized. You may also find that the inexperienced end users will quickly lose confidence in the system, while those who are more computer literate will try to short-circuit any support mechanisms that are in place. The result will be the use of *ad hoc* solutions, together with undocumented changes to the system — all of which only worsen the situation.

# Network Maintenance Log

Ref ID: MTC - 9301010001

| | | |
|---|---|---|
| ☐ System Login Script | ☐ Normal/Routine | |
| ☑ User Login Script | ☑ Trouble Resolution | |
| ☐ Gateways, Modems | | |
| ☐ Directory Structure(s) | | |
| ☐ Start-up Files/Configuration | | |
| ☐ Workstations | | |
| ☐ Bridges/Routers | | |
| ☐ Software Upgrades | | |
| ☐ NLM, Vaps, etc. | | |

Nature of Problem: User could not log in to system

☐ _____
☐ _____
☐ _____
☐ _____

*Nature of Changes*

| Ref. # | Description |
|---|---|
| 001 | User could not log in to main server. Problem due to corrupt login script file. |
| | Rebuilt file and tested.  Everything is now fine. |
| | |
| | |
| | |
| | |
| | |
| | |
| | |

Changed By:  Janet Lee                    On Date:93/08/17

Authorization:_____        Date:93/08/17

*Figure 6.2: Network Maintenance Log*

# Developing a Support Plan

Like most of the strategic operational plans, the support plan is developed primarily by the technology advisor. For the plan to be precise and detailed enough to be useful, several factors must be taken into consideration: the statement of support, the support team, the necessary tools, the related processes, technical support training, and the financial statement for the plan. Each of these is examined below.

## Statement of Support

The statement of support sums up all the support services relevant to the system, including those for system changes, software problems, and interventions. It also describes how these support services are to be provided — both basic services such as telephone hot lines and on-site assistance, and site-specific services in cases where the implementation covers several locations.

## Support Team

This part of the support plan provides details about the requisite support team, which is not part of the project team and is usually assigned during the later stages of the implementation. Unless your organization is in a position to assign specific resources to support, this task will be relegated to a third party.

The following points should be considered in this section of the support plan:

- Outsourcing, that is, requirements for third-party involvement

- Roles and responsibilities — who does what

- Requisite skill sets

- Lines of responsibility (reporting lines)

- Resource plan

## Tools

This section itemizes and describes all the tools required in an effective support plan, including these:

- Communication tools such as forms, reports, and so on

- Automated tracking tools such as databases

- Support team members' tools and test equipment, such as wire testers, diagnostic software, and so on

## Processes

This part of the support plan sets out the procedures and documentation required for the consistent handling of the following:

- The problem escalation process, including all documentation steps and the point at which inquiries should be forwarded from the LAN administrator to the hot line or third-party support

- The repair process, including who handles technical support, scheduling for technical support, and any equipment replacement agreements

- The routine and proactive maintenance processes, describing scheduling, documentation, and such responsibilities as monthly physical checks of all servers by the systems group or the vendor

- The handling and documentation of regular applications upgrades

- The schedule for site visits and consultation by the project team and the support team

## Technical Support Training

The support plan should provide specifications regarding the training of the technical support team, that is, anyone assigned the task of technical support. For example, if your systems group is to handle hot-line calls and some routine maintenance, the members might need to take certain product-specific courses offered by the vendor or another outside party.

The details given in this section, as in the rest of the support plan, will vary with your network solution. However, the section should include all curriculum information, the scheduling of training, the ordering process for training, and the outline of the baseline training program. It is important for this part of the support plan to be consistent with the LAN training plan for your technical support group.

### Financial Statement

The financial statement itemizes and totals all source funding and costs associated with the proposed support plan. It should provide detailed budget projections and allocations, a statement of attracted costs, and a complete financial analysis of the support plan. Developing the financial statement may be as straightforward as providing the necessary information on a single spreadsheet.

*************************

Once the support plan has been developed, it must be clearly communicated to both support staff and user groups as part of the overall LAN training process. Steps must also be taken to monitor its effectiveness, identify any areas needing change, and verify that the policies and procedures detailed in the plan are being followed. Again, like any strategic operational plan, the support plan must be reviewed and updated regularly.

## SYSTEM ACCEPTANCE TEST PLAN

The system acceptance test plan outlines the acceptance test plan for hardware and for the functional performance of system and application features. Your LAN implementation cannot be finalized without receiving this acceptance.

The first stage in developing a system acceptance test plan is to agree upon the criteria that constitute acceptance of the system by your organization. The task of defining acceptance criteria falls to the vendor selection committee, or to a group consisting of project team members and representatives of the user groups and the information systems group.

The system acceptance test plan, like all strategic operational plans, is specific to your LAN. It covers the following points:

- The features checklist, a detailed list of all components and features of your LAN

- What is to be tested

- The precise procedural steps to be followed in order to guarantee consistency in system acceptance testing

- The evaluation criteria agreed upon for system acceptance sign-off, audit, and accountability

System acceptance testing consists of a walk-through of the site by the LAN administrator and the project leader or technology advisor. During acceptance testing, the LAN administrator turns on and tests all LAN components designated in the system acceptance test plan. For example, to verify connectivity to a remote resource, the LAN administrator may log in at one workstation and attempt to make the connection.

System acceptance testing is done at the end of LAN installation (Phase III of the STEPS process). It is not to be confused with either of the more complete equipment testing processes which are undertaken and signed off on earlier, first at the end of pre-configuration and testing and again at installation testing. It is important to realize that acceptance at the end of Phase III does not imply formal system acceptance sign-off. This final acceptance does not occur until Phase IV, after your LAN has been in operation for at least two months. Chapter 11 provides details on the final sign-off.

## TRAINING PLAN

No matter how straightforward your implementation or applications may seem, they will not be successful unless your staff is trained. The purpose of the training plan is to bring about this success. The plan is based on the organization's corporate goals as well as the users' developmental needs and training objectives, including those specified in other strategic operational plans. When completed, the training plan will guide you in selecting, implementing, and evaluating appropriate training courses.

Each organization's training plan is uniquely suited to its own requirements. Regardless of the details, however, all LAN training plans have two distinct components, each one aimed at a different target audience: the LAN administrator and the end users.

It is the audience that determines the timing of training. The LAN administrator is trained before the end users, during Phase II, installation preparation. This intensive system administrator training often takes place at a vendor training facility. It may be undertaken by the technology advisor and the prime user group co-ordinator.

The training of the users usually does not come until Phase III, after the network is installed but before the post-installation review in Phase IV. Ideally, it is performed on site. The users' training schedules require co-ordination among the trainer, the prime user group co-ordinator, any necessary third parties, and the users themselves. If third-party training is called for, the technology advisor must see to it that the necessary funding approvals are in order and that procedural matters such as work orders and cheque requisitions have been taken care of. Figure 6.3 shows the two separate training audiences, and places their training in the context of the entire implementation.

Helping all employees maximize their knowledge of the new system and their benefit from it may be done in two ways, through formal instruction or informal training. **Formal instruction** requires an instructor, and has an identifiable structure designed to develop an individual's occupational skills. It may be carried out on the job or in a classroom setting, on or off site, during or after work hours — in whichever combination is most appropriate. **Informal training** is provided by a more experienced fellow worker or a supervisor of the trainee, and is always done on the job during normal hours. It is often referred to as an apprentice program. Both formal instruction and informal training are equally valid; which approach is chosen depends on the individual situation.

The discussion below provides a guide to the items which must be considered in developing an effective training plan. It should also help you verify that your organization's training needs are being met. This is not to say, however, that you should omit retaining an experienced outside instructor or designating a trainer from your project team.

## Assessing Training Needs

Both the assessment of training needs and the development of a training plan for LAN implementation are ultimately the responsibility of the technology advisor. Depending upon the extent and complexity of the project, the task may be undertaken by the technology advisor or delegated to others, whether in-house or outside resources. When training needs are assessed, the two target audiences of the training plan — the LAN administrator and the end users — should be kept clearly in mind.

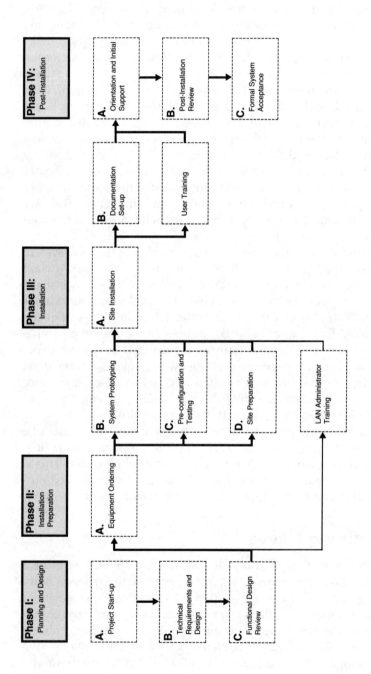

*Figure 6.3: Training as Part of the LAN Implementation Process*

Assessing training needs is a fairly straightforward process which forms part of the needs analysis study discussed in Chapter 2. The information about training requirements is obtained from the completed needs assessment matrices and end user profile worksheets. To be truly valuable, this information should be extrapolated six to twelve months ahead. Also included in the needs analysis are all relevant organizational needs, as identified in the corporate information technology strategic plan. Whether your organization's training needs are many or few, you will find the training needs assessment helpful in the planning, selection, implementation, and evaluation of training programs and/or courses.

To organize the information about training needs, you could again use a structured format which examines the following topics: an introductory overview; a summary of the situation; organizational and situational objectives; the positions affected; the knowledge and skills required; individual trainee requirements; training delivery considerations; and evaluation procedures. Each of these points is discussed in turn below.

## Introduction

This section of the training needs assessment presents an overview of the recent history of the organization, focusing on products, services, number of employees, and structure. The position of the business within the marketplace is discussed, with reference to anticipated growth or decline, the effects of competition, and the available labour supply. Past situations involving training should also be outlined here.

## Summary of the Situation

This section delineates the issues relevant to the situation at hand, whether changes, problems, or interventions. It also comments on their anticipated effects on the organization. Because of the time and resources required for developing a training course and for training itself, it is necessary to project six to twelve months ahead.

Each situation should be treated on an individual basis. As an example, suppose that improvements — the introduction of robotics and of a related LAN software application — are being made to an assembly line in a factory. The reasons why training is required in the use of the new equipment and software must be identified and noted in the situation summary. A statement regarding potential consequences of not providing training must also be included.

## *Organizational and Situational Objectives*

In this section, all organizational objectives must be identified. Each should be considered in light of the following factors:

- Attributes

- Unit of measure

- Target

- Scheduling

The organizational goals should be related to the coming twelve-month period. If the analysis is done properly, it should be possible to relate each organizational goal directly to the issues set out in the situation summary. It is important to keep in mind that training is not the only consideration in this analysis; situational issues are also of prime importance. For example, assume that the factory mentioned above is introducing robotics in order to meet the organizational goal of expanding production output by 10% over the next one-year period. Depending on the skill sets of the workers, they may or may not require training to meet this objective. The second organizational goal would involve the introduction of the related LAN software application. The users would require basic LAN training in order to meet the objective of becoming conversant with the network — requiring minimal telephone support — by the end of the same period.

## *Positions Affected*

This section identifies the job positions in the organization which will be affected when each organizational and situational objective listed in the previous section is met. It also provides a brief job description listing key responsibilities for each position affected. Finally, for each job description, it enumerates all anticipated changes in performance or behaviour which should follow training.

For example, suppose that plant supervisor Janet Lee is being trained in basic word processing and electronic mail usage. The expectation is that, after training, she will be capable of creating and responding directly to her own in-house correspondence, which she is not presently able to do.

### Requisite Knowledge and Skills

This section lists the knowledge and skills in which each employee will require training, in order to demonstrate the specific performances or behaviours associated with each job position listed in the previous section (Positions Affected). Any prerequisite knowledge and skills which the employees should have before being trained in the use of the new system, such as a working knowledge of MS-DOS, Windows, databases, and the like, should also be listed.

### Individual Trainee Requirements

This section lists all the employees filling each job position identified in the section Positions Affected. Each employee is then assessed against the relevant situational objective to verify that there is a relationship. Where a relationship exists, a match must be made between the employee and the knowledge and skills he or she will require to contribute actively to the objective. Again, any prerequisite knowledge and skills are to be included for each worker.

For an illustration, let us turn again to the example of the factory discussed above. The workers on the assembly line where robotics and a related LAN software application are to be introduced may fall into a number of categories:

- The employees who presently work on the assembly line and have no experience in working with robotics; these will require basic training.

- Those who currently work on the assembly line and have some experience in working with robotics; these will require refresher courses and/or management training.

- Employees who do not currently work on the assembly line which is being upgraded but may be moved there because they have some experience with robotics; these will require either basic or refresher courses.

Once the workers are divided into these categories, the process is repeated to find the level of computer literacy among them. In this way, it can be determined whether the requisite LAN training needs to be preceded by any preliminary computer courses.

The information gathered should be summarized in the form of an assessment matrix. The matrix will clearly indicate which employees already have some level of knowledge or prerequisite skills, and what type of further training they require; which workers have no relevant knowledge and skills, and must be provided with introductory training; and which workers might best be redirected to other tasks.

## *Training Delivery Considerations*

In this section, each of these issues should be raised and discussed:

- Is funding for training available?

- Where will training sessions be held?

- How many hours per week can the organization afford to invest in training?

- When can workers be released for training purposes during regular work hours, and when can they not?

- Which instructional method would be better suited to the organization's needs, formal instruction or informal training?

- Should training materials be developed in-house, or is an appropriate off-the-shelf training course available?

- What equipment is needed for training: overhead projectors and transparencies, slide projectors and slides, VCRs, etc.?

## *Evaluation Procedures*

This section identifies the individual(s) within the organization who will be responsible for evaluating training. This task usually falls to the project team's trainer, or some combination of information systems staff and human resources specialists. If an outside training consultant has assisted in developing the training plan, he or she may also become involved in establishing the evaluation criteria. These criteria are established according to the training which is to be evaluated, and are set out in this part of the training plan as well. Finally, the section states when evaluation will occur.

## Developing a Training Plan

As indicated earlier, ultimate responsibility for the training plan rests with the technology advisor. The actual development of the plan, however, is the joint responsibility of the trainer and the participants. This approach guarantees that all necessary information will be available for assessment and inclusion in the final training plan. If your organization has a human resources department or other staff with the skills needed in the development of the training plan, the technology advisor may delegate this task, in part or entirely, to these individuals.

The training plan provides guidelines for the following matters:

- Control and direction in communicating expectations about training

- Control of the process of selecting cost-effective, high-quality instruction

- Structure for the delivery of training, in order to cause minimum disruption and attain maximum effectiveness

- Establishment of the training process, so that it may be reviewed and its success may be measured

Depending on the size and complexity of the implementation, more than one training plan may be required in order to meet the training needs identified.

The first step in developing the training plan is to write the training solution. This document sets out the proposed solution to the training requirements identified during assessment. It is a customized approach to addressing those requirements, and provides the information needed for planning, selecting, implementing, and evaluating any training. When the training solution is finalized, a conclusion is added to it, whereupon it becomes the training plan.

Like the training needs assessment, the training solution is best organized in a structured way, in terms of the following topics: summary; training objectives; instruction methods and evaluation procedures; instructor's qualifications; equipment, location, and time; and a financial statement. As mentioned above, these six sections are followed up with a conclusion.

## Summary

This section of the training solution outlines the proposed training and should address all of these matters:

- Modules or topics, with detailed outlines for each

- Hours per module

- Total number of hours of training

- Number of trainees

- Class size

- Schedule

## Training Objectives

This section states precisely what each trainee will be expected to have learned and what he or she will be able to do as a result of the training. These objectives will reflect the training requirements set out in the assessment of training needs. Each objective must also be directly related to one or more of the situational objectives identified in the Organizational and Situational Objectives section of the assessment.

## Instruction Methods and Evaluation Procedures

This section details the methodology of the instruction, and explains why undertaking the training is appropriate for the organization. It also describes the evaluation procedures to be used, and establishes how the progress of each trainee will be appraised during and after the training program, e.g., tests, reviews, assignments, etc.

## Instructor's Qualifications

Unless your organization has its own training resources, or the task is very large, the instructor(s) will come from outside. This section of the training solution lists all relevant characteristics and qualifications of an instructor:

- Educational background

- Previous training experience

- A list of references familiar with the instructor's training experience

A copy of the instructor's résumé may also be included.

### Equipment, Location, and Time

All materials, supplies, and other equipment necessary for training are itemized here. Also stated are the location where the training sessions are to be held, and the time of each session.

### Financial Statement

The financial statement for the training solution itemizes and totals all costs associated with the proposed training. Again, a spreadsheet may be used for generating the financial statement. The following points should be covered in the statement:

- Direct cost of instruction per hour

- Itemized cost of supplies, materials, and other equipment

- Rental or leasing costs

- Travel and accommodation expenses

### Conclusion

When both the training needs assessment and the training solution have been completed, a conclusion tying the two documents together is added to the latter. This final section of the training solution is a summary of the proposed training approach. Applied correctly, it will help you develop an effective training plan, either within your organization or in conjunction with an outside training consultant. The resulting plan may recommend a customized approach specific to your organization, or an off-the-shelf training course. In either case, the final training plan should address the following:

- Organizational objectives

- Training methods

- Expected training results

- Evaluation procedures

- The connection between objectives and results

- All costs, resources, and necessary organizational commitment to the proposed training plan

- A list of the equipment required

- Details on funding for the training program

The guidelines set out above should be effective in developing a LAN-oriented training plan. However, be careful never to lose sight of the following LAN-specific requirements:

- Regardless of the size of the implementation, you must have a training plan.

- The training plan must address the needs of the end users — the majority of the trainees.

- The plan must also address the LAN administrator's needs.

- The training requirements of these groups — LAN administrator and end users — will normally be quite different.

- In general, the two groups should be trained at different times.

- It is a good idea to begin assessing training needs during the needs analysis study, to save both time and effort.

# FINANCIAL PLAN

The financial plan details the budgetary costs of the LAN implementation. All the financial statements associated with other strategic operational plans, such as the support plan and the training plan, must be included in the overall financial plan.

Like other financial analyses, the financial plan will be presented in the format preferred by your organization. Whatever form it takes, it must include two major sections, one entitled Financial Assumptions, the other, Detailed Cost Breakdown. The first of these itemizes all working assumptions upon which the detailed cost breakdown is based. The Detailed Cost Breakdown section is normally presented as a printout from a spreadsheet. It shows both capital and operating costs required for the implementation and maintenance of your LAN installation. Capital costs include such categories as hardware/equipment, software, cabling, installation, and miscellaneous items. Operating costs cover financial/administrative expenses, equipment leases, and all support costs. They are generally broken down by quarter and given for a two-year period. With today's rapidly changing technology and business environment, a two-year view is normally considered adequate.

The financial plan is a critical component of the system solution report. It must have management approval for the SSR to obtain sign-off authorization.

*************************

The strategic operational plans are both essential and complementary to your system design. The development of customized strategic operational plans will help to ensure that your LAN will operate effectively, once implementation is complete.

# PART TWO

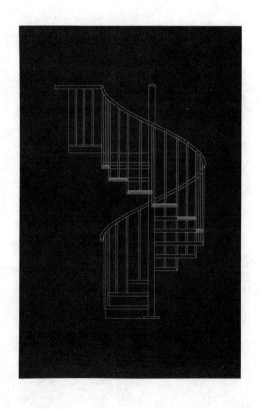

# 7

AN OVERVIEW OF THE STEPS
PROCESS AND STEPS: TOOLS

# CHAPTER 7

# AN OVERVIEW OF THE STEPS PROCESS AND STEPS: TOOLS

It has already been pointed out that the purpose of the STEPS process is to demystify a highly technical undertaking and provide you with a methodology that will enhance your ability to succeed in the implementation of a LAN. Like any change in a business, a LAN implementation must be planned with care. The adoption and clear understanding of an effective, well-documented approach are essential for minimizing organizational disruptions. Whether or not you have a technical background, the systematic process offered by STEPS will supply the necessary combination of information, direction, and tools to make your implementation manageable. Together, the STEPS process and STEPS: Tools will allow you to apply the same basic principles of planning, analysis, and control to the implementation of virtually any LAN.

This chapter provides an overview of both the STEPS process, introduced in Chapter 1, and STEPS: Tools. These two interrelated topics are the focus of the remaining chapters of this book. The STEPS process consists of four phases, which form a tested series of activities comprised of a variety of interdependent tasks. The value of the process lies in its ability to accomplish the following:

• Provide a means for organizing information about the implementation in a consistent manner

- Improve accountability throughout the project by providing an audit of sign-offs at both the worksheet and the report approval levels

- Provide a mechanism whereby the project team can progressively achieve accurate, approved documentation

STEPS: Tools is a series of project management process charts, forms, and reports which is directly related to the activities of the STEPS process. It is intended, not only as organized documentation, but also as a control mechanism which, when used according to instructions, provides the checks and balances to let you pull your entire implementation together and make it a success.

You may find that Chapters 8 - 11 read much like a procedural manual. In many ways, that is exactly what they are. The level of explanation, however, is specifically directed at management. If you find the discussion of some parts of the process highly technical, it is so by necessity. As mentioned in earlier chapters, technical information has been included not to give you the details for personally undertaking the task, but rather to make you aware of the nature of the tasks involved, their relationship to one another, and the delegation of responsibility for each task.

To obtain the greatest benefit from Part Two, you will find it very useful to read through Part One, if you have not done so already. Together with the Glossary, Chapters 1 - 6 should provide enough background to let you easily follow the flow of events and accountabilities in the STEPS process.

# **H**OW TO USE THE STEPS PROCESS

From the summary provided in Chapter 1, you are already somewhat familiar with the four phases of the STEPS process: planning and design, installation preparation, installation, and post-installation. Figure 7.1 shows each phase in relation to the others, and in terms of the various activities to be accomplished. Each of Chapters 8 - 11 covers one of the phases in depth.

As you make your way through Part Two, you will find each phase of LAN implementation depicted in a series of process charts, also known as **PERT charts**. (The acronym PERT stands for program evaluation and review technique.) The charts offer a graphic view of the various activities, procedures, and tasks which make up each phase. The hierarchy and process lines denote the related dependencies. Starting at

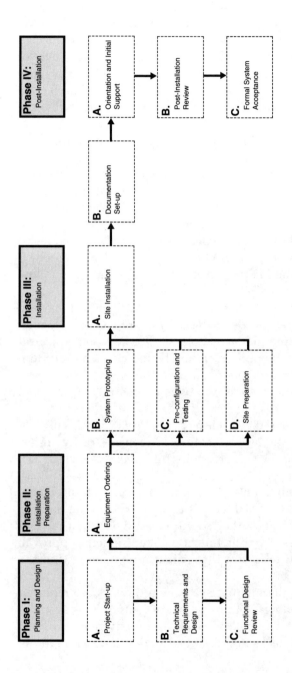

*Figure 7.1: The Four Phases of the STEPS Process, and Dependent Activities*

Figure 7.1, you can "walk through" each phase of the process — and all the levels of work it involves — by scanning the appropriate detail-level process charts and reading the accompanying discussions within the text.

It is important to note that, for the sake of clarity, the top level of work within each phase is always referred to as an *activity*. Thus, Figure 7.1 tells you that there are 12 activities which make up the STEPS process. The next level of work is always called a *procedure*, while the third and lowest level is a *task*.

As an illustration, consider Phase I of the STEPS process, planning and design, shown at the far left of Figure 7.1. You can see that Phase I consists of three activities: project start-up (A), technical requirements and design (B), and functional design review (C). Note that each activity is assigned a letter. In Chapter 8, Phase I: Planning and Design, there is a detailed process chart for each of these three activities. The chart for each activity is further broken down into its constituent procedures and tasks. Figure 7.2 duplicates the first process chart found in Chapter 8, which shows the first activity in the STEPS process, in order to help you follow the explanation below more easily.

You can see from Figure 7.2 that this first activity, project start-up (A), involves five procedures: needs analysis (1), planning and organizing the project (2), completing the project plan (3), project plan approval (4), and the project start-up announcement (5). Note that each procedure is assigned a number. To make the sequence even easier to follow, procedures are always placed in shadow boxes across the top of each process chart.

Figure 7.2 further reveals that each of procedures 1 - 5 involves a number of tasks. For example, needs analysis (1) consists of five tasks: assigning the project leader (1.1), performing the needs analysis (1.2), developing the functional requirements specification document (1.3), presenting functional requirements (1.4), and functional requirements approval (1.5). As you can see, each task is assigned a decimal number on the basis of its sequence within the procedure. Also note that the first four tasks are in plain boxes; the fifth, functional requirements approval, is in a double box, which tells you that it is a milestone within the STEPS process.

The letter and number pertaining to each item of work are repeated beside the appropriate headings within the text of Chapter 8 — again, to make the sequence simpler to follow. The three activities and their dependent procedures and tasks are described in depth, each under its own heading.

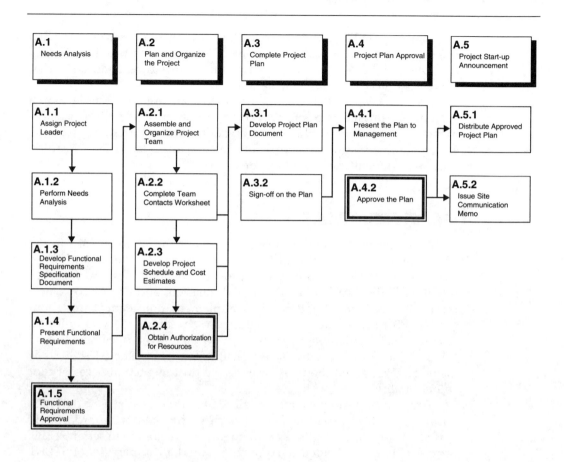

*Figure 7.2: STEPS: Process Chart for Phase I, Activity A — Project Start-up*

Chapters 9 - 11 go on to examine the other three phases of the STEPS process in the same detailed manner. This approach provides a truly step-by-step guideline to all the activities, procedures, and tasks that make up a successful implementation.

Each process chart is intended to help your organization develop a customized implementation. Working with automated project management software (though this is not essential) and information from the early planning sessions, the project team customizes task lists, schedules, durations, dependencies, and responsibilities.

# THE STEPS: TOOLS

As you read the in-depth descriptions of the various tasks in the STEPS process, you will find frequent references to schedules, forms, worksheets, studies, reports, and approvals. Together these items constitute the STEPS: Tools which provide a consistent and organized control mechanism and audit trail for your implementation team. Throughout the STEPS process, acceptance is directly related to accountability. Accountability is demonstrated by sign-off on a given document, which stands as a record of who is responsible for what. The STEPS: Tools included throughout the book provide the documentation necessary for accountability.

You will find sample copies of all STEPS: Process Charts and STEPS: Forms, as well as a framework for each STEPS: Report appropriately placed within each chapter. For easy reference, a complete set of STEPS: Process Charts is included in Appendix A, and a complete set of STEPS: Forms can be found in Appendix B. This latter appendix also cross-references each form with the activity or activities within which it is used.

Details on the various studies, reports, and required approvals mentioned in Part Two are given throughout this book. Wherever possible, they have been referenced for your ease of use. Keep in mind, though, that it will be a project team member with the requisite skill sets who uses many of them. Specifics about individual forms and worksheets and sign-off authorizations will be self-explanatory for this individual. These tools are included here to let you see and audit the overall flow of events, as well as for the project team's reference.

While all of the STEPS: Tools (STEPS: Process Charts, STEPS: Forms, and STEPS: Reports) can be used effectively as they appear in this book, they are also available in automated form for use on your personal computer. You can order the STEPS: Tools software by using the fulfillment card at the back of this book.

Details on the three elements of STEPS: Tools are provided below, with an explanation of how they can be useful to your LAN implementation — whether you use them as they appear in this book, or in the electronic version.

## STEPS: Process Charts

The STEPS: Process Charts found in Part Two of this book are project templates (.mpp files) created on Microsoft Project for Windows. As mentioned earlier, the generic copies of the charts included in the book provide a guideline for the customization of the STEPS process to your implementation. You can assign your own resources, adjust the tasks and dependencies if need be, and generate your organization's project-specific PERT and Gantt charts, to provide graphic views of tasks and dependencies. (A **Gantt chart** shows project schedules and is used for tracking; for further information, refer to the Glossary. An example of a Gantt chart appears in Figure 7.3.)

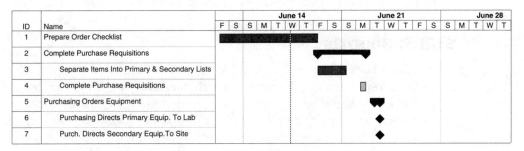

| ID | Name | | | | | | | | | | | | | | | | | | | | | | |
|----|------|--|--|--|--|--|--|--|--|--|--|--|--|--|--|--|--|--|--|--|--|--|
| | | F | S | S | M | T | W | T | F | S | S | M | T | W | T | F | S | S | M | T | W | T |
| 1 | Prepare Order Checklist | | | | | | | | | | | | | | | | | | | | | |
| 2 | Complete Purchase Requisitions | | | | | | | | | | | | | | | | | | | | | |
| 3 | Separate Items Into Primary & Secondary Lists | | | | | | | | | | | | | | | | | | | | | |
| 4 | Complete Purchase Requisitions | | | | | | | | | | | | | | | | | | | | | |
| 5 | Purchasing Orders Equipment | | | | | | | | | | | | | | | | | | | | | |
| 6 | Purchasing Directs Primary Equip. To Lab | | | | | | | | | | | | | | | | | | | | | |
| 7 | Purch. Directs Secondary Equip.To Site | | | | | | | | | | | | | | | | | | | | | |

*Figure 7.3: Gantt Chart for Equipment Ordering*

If you order the STEPS: Tools software, the ready-made files can be loaded into Microsoft Project and customized electronically to your specific environment. You can also create various reports and views on resource usage and costs, using the features built into Microsoft Project.

However your PERT and Gantt charts are developed, they are distributed and reviewed to ensure that all tasks and schedules are agreed upon and all responsibilities are assigned. These charts are integral to maintaining sign-off and accountability during your implementation.

## STEPS: Forms

The STEPS: Forms (.frp files) were developed on DELRINA PerForm PRO. Using the forms described and provided in the book, you can organize and audit the various tasks of the implementation process as they are dealt with. The end result is the creation of a customized set of documentation which helps in tracking and maintaining all your LAN-related information, both during the implementation and afterwards. You will find this material is especially important for ongoing service and support.

When loaded into DELRINA PerForm PRO Plus Filler, the STEPS: Forms component of the STEPS: Tools software automatically generates industry-standard ASCII and .dbf format database files. These files are compatible with most PC-based database software packages. Thanks to this capability, as you fill in the forms electronically, you are entering information into a database. The resulting customized, automated documentation enhances your ability to keep all information about your LAN up to date. If you wish to customize the STEPS: Forms even further — e.g., enter your company logo, set default information, customize database fields, etc. — fax your request along with the enclosed fulfillment card. Any such alterations should be completed before the forms are used.

## STEPS: Reports

The STEPS: Reports, based primarily on the STEPS: Forms, provide a built-in reporting mechanism used throughout the implementation process. The three most important reports, which were introduced in Chapter 1, are the site inspection report (SIR), the system solution report (SSR), and the site upgrade requirements report (SURR). All of them are essential for management control, since each is a critical deliverable that must be presented, approved, and signed off on. An overview of the reports is provided below, as each one is central to the entire implementation. The SSR in particular is referred to and updated throughout the STEPS process.

The site inspection report gives details about the organization's current operating environment in both functional and physical terms. To develop this report, the project team must collect and summarize a great deal of diverse information. The team members will soon come to appreciate the value of using the STEPS: Forms, which provide a complete, consistent, and organized format for this task. Moreover, if they are working with the electronic version of the forms, they will be in a position to create and continually update a project-specific set of documentation — a definite asset, particularly in a large, complex, or problematic implementation.

The system solution report is the next major deliverable of the STEPS process. It combines the details in the site inspection report with the information in other STEPS: Forms and design information, to document the proposed design and system solution. As discussed in Chapter 6, the strategic operational plans for the LAN implementation are important components of the SSR. The report provides the fundamental documentation which will be referred to throughout the STEPS process. It will need to be continually updated and approved, should any changes result from application pilots, testing, or installation. All tasks which follow the approval of the SSR come back to this document.

Once the SIR and the SSR are approved, they are used to generate a list of items which must be changed for the LAN site to be able to accommodate the approved solution. These changes are documented by means of the STEPS: Forms, and presented as the site upgrade requirements report. This document details all the physical site requirements that must be addressed before installation, their cost, and target dates for completion of the work.

All three reports must be approved for Phase I of the LAN implementation to be considered complete. To give proper approval, both technical and managerial staff must carefully study the solution being proposed and undertaken. These individuals assume responsibility for their decision by providing their sign-offs. The approved system solution report represents the authorized solution. It is through the use and approval of the three reports — and of the many others involved in the STEPS process — that accountability is guaranteed throughout the implementation.

As mentioned earlier in the chapter, the key authorizations and milestones associated with the STEPS process are double-boxed in the various process charts, to help you in locating them.

PHASE I: PLANNING AND
DESIGN

• • • • • • • • • • • • • • • • • • •

# CHAPTER 8

# PHASE I: PLANNING AND DESIGN

The first phase of the STEPS process is in many ways the most criti-cal. Having made the decision to implement a LAN, your organization must now undertake the work that lays the foundation for the project. Regardless of how straightforward or complex the anticipated require-ments of your LAN may be, the quality of the preparatory work and start-up has a direct bearing on the effectiveness and ease with which your implementation will be managed.

It is at this phase that you will begin to rely on the features offered by STEPS: Tools. Its various components are designed to assist in the management, organization, and documentation of your implementation. STEPS: Tools provides a tested approach to the control and audit of all necessary tasks, reports, and sign-off authorizations.

This is also the time when you will investigate the needs of both the business and the end users, and establish those details which will distin-guish your LAN requirements from those of other organizations. If you follow the STEPS process and develop the requisite material as described, then you will have created a reliable audit of all tasks as well as a set of documentation tailored to your LAN by the time implementation is com-plete. More immediately, at the end of Phase I you will have the three key deliverables discussed in previous chapters: the site inspection report, the system solution report, and the site upgrade requirements report. They are developed in the course of the lengthy but necessary planning process, and must be reviewed and approved before authorization is given for the project to proceed to the implementation itself.

In Chapter 7, you were introduced to the organization of this chapter and the remaining three chapters of the book, each of which deals with one phase of the STEPS process. Recall that each chapter is broken down by the activities involved in each phase, as shown in Figure 7.1 on page 109. Chapter 8 therefore has three main sections: Project Start-up, Technical Requirements and Design, and Functional Design Review. As mentioned in Chapter 7, each of these activities is accompanied by a process chart and is further subdivided according to the dependent procedures and tasks required for the completion of the activity. You are now ready to commence following the STEPS process, with the assistance of this literally step-by-step guideline to all the tasks involved in a successful implementation.

## A.  P ROJECT START-UP

Many people performing a great variety of activities are likely to take part in a LAN implementation. It is essential to begin the project by taking an organized approach to the selection and management of the people involved. It is also vital to cultivate a sense of ownership of the project on the part of both management and the users, from the very start.

Figure 8.1 shows that the first activity in Phase I, project start-up, involves five procedures: needs analysis, planning and organizing the project, completing the project plan, project plan approval, and the project start-up announcement. They will be examined in turn below, in light of the tasks to be completed during each procedure.

## A.1  Needs Analysis

The first procedure associated with the start-up of LAN implementation is undertaking a needs analysis. Figure 8.1 reveals that it is comprised of five tasks: assigning the project leader, performing the needs analysis, developing the functional requirements specification document, presenting the functional requirements, and functional requirements approval. Each is discussed in turn below.

Because this stage of an implementation is so critical to its success, all of Chapter 2 is also devoted to needs analysis.

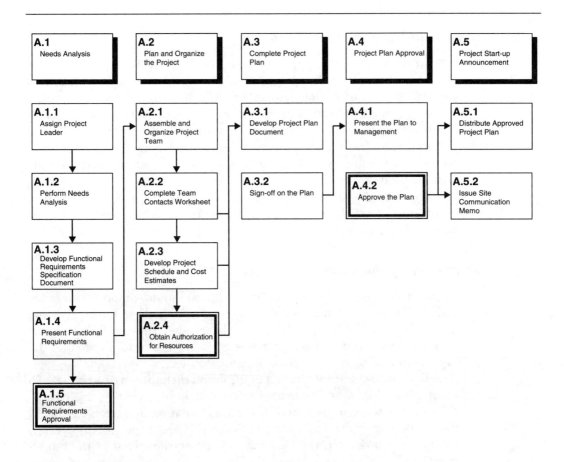

| A.1 | A.2 | A.3 | A.4 | A.5 |
|---|---|---|---|---|
| Needs Analysis | Plan and Organize the Project | Complete Project Plan | Project Plan Approval | Project Start-up Announcement |

| A.1.1 | A.2.1 | A.3.1 | A.4.1 | A.5.1 |
|---|---|---|---|---|
| Assign Project Leader | Assemble and Organize Project Team | Develop Project Plan Document | Present the Plan to Management | Distribute Approved Project Plan |

| A.1.2 | A.2.2 | A.3.2 | A.4.2 | A.5.2 |
|---|---|---|---|---|
| Perform Needs Analysis | Complete Team Contacts Worksheet | Sign-off on the Plan | Approve the Plan | Issue Site Communication Memo |

**A.1.3** Develop Functional Requirements Specification Document

**A.2.3** Develop Project Schedule and Cost Estimates

**A.1.4** Present Functional Requirements

**A.2.4** Obtain Authorization for Resources

**A.1.5** Functional Requirements Approval

*Figure 8.1: STEPS: Process Chart for Phase I, Activity A — Project Start-up*

### A.1.1    Assigning the Project Leader

To undertake your organization's needs analysis, a project leader must be chosen. Ideally, this individual will see the implementation through from start to finish, together with the project team. The project leader can be an in-house staff member or an outside third party, such as a consultant, contractor, or vendor representative. Chapters 2 and 3 give details about the rationale and timing for selecting both the project leader and the team members, as well as the duties associated with the various positions.

You should be aware that the selection of the project team may occur at various points during project start-up. It may occur at this time, or later in the start-up process.

### A.1.2    Performing the Needs Analysis

Once the project leader has been selected, an orientation session (or series of sessions) is held for the end users. After these meetings come the in-depth planning meetings which are the true beginning of the needs analysis study. This research is performed in order to identify the organization's needs. Corporate information technology plans are integrated with the identified needs of all users, including management. To accomplish this, a fairly standard series of issues must be addressed. These matters are to be found in the functional requirements specification outline and the end user profile worksheets (refer to Chapter 2), which must now be completed for each person involved in the implementation. The purpose of all this fact-finding is to identify and document your business needs, as well as the opportunities and risks associated with different information technology solutions.

For your implementation to succeed, a sense of involvement must exist on the part of both management and end users. The end user orientation and planning sessions (discussed in Chapter 2) promote this much-needed feeling.

### A.1.3    Developing the Functional Requirements Specification Document

After all information related to needs analysis — including the needs assessment matrix — has been assembled, the functional requirements specification document can be developed. This task falls to either the project leader or the technology advisor. The functional requirements specification document is an explicit statement of requirements which must precede the technical design of your system solution. Its details must respond to the inquiries of both the functional requirements specification outline and the information systems detail inquiries (found in Chapter 2 on pages 20 - 21 and 22 - 23, respectively).

### A.1.4    Presenting the Functional Requirements

The functional requirements specification document must be presented to management for approval. The details of how the presentation is developed and to whom it is made vary with each organization.

 *Functional Requirements Approval*

Obtaining management approval for the functional requirements specification document is the first milestone of the STEPS process. Like the method of presenting the document, the manner in which the requirements are reviewed and formal approvals are given varies with the corporate directives of each organization.

# A.2    Planning and Organizing the Project

This second procedure in the start-up process has four component tasks: assembling and organizing the project team, completing the team contacts worksheet, developing the project schedule and cost estimates, and obtaining authorization for resources.

### A.2.1    Assembling and Organizing the Project Team

As noted earlier, the project team may be chosen at the same time as the project leader, or at another point during project start-up. The timing is related to the specifics of the needs analysis in your organization and is covered in more detail in Chapters 2 and 3.

In any case, once the project team has been selected, the project leader carefully allots tasks according to each team member's skill set. The project team's project management practices are detailed at this stage of the process. Discussions are held to clarify any questions about the members' respective roles and responsibilities. Next, the project team establishes the following:

- How the project will be organized

- What the project's objectives are

- What constitutes viable resource requirements, task assignments, target delivery dates, and schedules

These concerns are most easily dealt with by using the automated STEPS: Project Templates. Communication methods and lines of authority are also established before the project team moves on to the work at hand.

Throughout the delivery cycle, there are many tasks to be accomplished. The project team must be able to complete all the steps of planning, reporting, and obtaining approvals which are needed to make the implementation a success.

## A.2.2    Completing the Team Contacts Worksheet

To help the team members communicate among themselves, the **team contacts worksheet** is completed and distributed. This document identifies all members of the project team and the supporting resource people, and gives their telephone numbers. A sample team contacts worksheet is shown in Figure 8.2.

## A.2.3    Developing the Project Schedule and Cost Estimates

The detailed process charts given for the 12 activities in the STEPS process are designed for a generic implementation. Nonetheless, they will be of considerable help in developing a customized schedule or timeline for your implementation.

You may find it a fairly complex undertaking to install a new system and train the end users. With the help of the process charts, you can tailor the details of the implementation to your organization. Items related to your specific requirements can easily be deleted or added. For instance, suppose your organization has a unique purchasing process. Therefore, your project team will probably need to add certain tasks having to do with purchasing and the related dependencies and dates to the generic equipment ordering process chart. Though it is not necessary, using the automated STEPS project management software generally speeds up the customization.

# Team Contacts Worksheet

Ref ID: TM - TCW9301010001

Project Name: NYSALESBRANCHLAN

Project ID: 930001-00

Organization Name:  IT Support

Key Contact:  Bob Esbin

Phone #: AAA-BBBB

## Participant Members

| Name | Title | Office Location | Phone # | Role(s) |
|---|---|---|---|---|
| George Nadas | Mgr. IT Support | NY Head Office | AAA-BBBB | Project Leader |
| Josh Rosenberg | Sr. Business Consultant,HQ.Systems | NY Head Office | AAA-BBBB | Technology Adv. |
| Ariel Winslow | Administrative Assistant | NY Head Office | AAA-BBBB | Project Admin. |
| Gino Ruffo | Installation Specialist, IT Support | NY Head Office | AAA-BBBB | Install. Specialist |
| Scott Maavara | Training Manager, HQ Info Resources | NY Head Office | AAA-BBBB | Trainer |
| | | | | |
| | | | | |
| | | | | |
| | | | | |
| | | | | |
| | | | | |
| | | | | |
| | | | | |

## Supporting Groups

| Group Name | Key Contacts | Phone # | Role(s) | Notes |
|---|---|---|---|---|
| HQ Engineering | Doug Hylton | 555-1212 | Tech. Design | Reports to Mike |
| Cable Systems Design Inc. | Ian Hindsmith | 555-XXXX | Cable Installer | On contract |
| Able Telecom Inc. | Guy Marchand | 416-555-1212 | Phone Co. | Sales rep. |
| | | | | |
| | | | | |
| | | | | |
| | | | | |

*Figure 8.2: Team Contacts Worksheet*

When completed, the customized PERT and Gantt charts are stapled to a copy of the team contacts worksheet. The project leader obtains agreement and accountability by circulating this package to the entire team for acceptance. Each team member is required to sign off on his or her responsibilities, date the signature, and return the package to the leader. This sign-off — just one of many yet to come — stands as a record of who is responsible for what. An initial from each team member goes a long way towards holding each participant to a commitment, should priorities change during the project.

 **Obtaining Authorization for Resources**

In large projects, it is usually necessary for the team to obtain written authorization and commitment from management, so that staff resources may be allocated to the project. A signed and dated copy of the project schedule normally provides an adequate explanation of roles and responsibilities for obtaining authorization and commitment. The written commitment from management for each project resource — whether staff or otherwise — serves as an audit of accountability and helps to ensure that all resources are available when needed. It is also the second milestone in the STEPS process.

## A.3    Completing the Project Plan

Completion of the project plan involves two tasks: developing the project plan document, and signing off on the plan.

### A.3.1    Developing the Project Plan Document

Before implementation can be started, management must receive a project plan. This plan, drawn up by the project team, lists all the tasks which must be done for the objectives to be achieved, along with target dates for each one. It also states all deliverables, together with the associated target dates. In addition, the project plan specifies the tasks to be performed by the organization.

Every deliverable listed in the project plan is associated with a management sign-off. Incremental sign-off is much less threatening to the organization than is waiting until the end of the project to sign off on the entire system. Another advantage of this approach is that, at the end of the implementation, the LAN site managers will feel that they received exactly what they thought they were getting.

The project plan generally contains these elements:

CHECK
LIST

✔ Executive summary

✔ Project methodology summary

✔ A summary of project communication, control, and reporting mechanisms

✔ Signed project schedules

✔ Assumptions regarding the project budget and cost estimates

✔ Project control forms and instructions (one copy of each)

### A.3.2 Signing Off on the Plan

Before the project plan is presented to the managers of the site user group, it must be signed off on by the project team. Then, after the various deliverables, tasks, and resources listed in the plan have been agreed upon, the project leader and the information systems managers sign off on it.

## A.4 Project Plan Approval

Once the project plan has been signed off on, it must be approved. Two tasks are involved here: presenting the plan to management, and approving the plan.

### A.4.1 Presenting the Plan to Management

Now that the project team, project leader, and information systems managers have signed off on the project plan, it is ready to be presented to site management. Depending on the scale of the project and the organization, this exercise may or may not be straightforward. In the case of a large organization or a complex implementation, it may be necessary to develop and deliver a number of presentations before final approval can be obtained for the project plan.

## Approving the Plan

Obtaining approval for the project plan is the third milestone in the implementation. By the time the plan is presented to management, there should be a single manager — the prime user group co-ordinator — who is responsible for signing off on all project deliverables. Like any project, a LAN implementation can be extremely difficult to manage and obtain approval for when a committee is involved.

### PROJECT STATUS REPORT

The ultimate responsibility for delivering the project on time and within budget rests with the project leader. An effective vehicle for analysing and controlling projects is the **project status report**. You can see a completed example in Figure 8.3.

The project leader will likely complete the first project status report after the project plan has been approved, and for each subsequent status review meeting. Depending on the scale of the project, these sessions may be held weekly, biweekly, or monthly. The prime user group co-ordinator should sign off on the report at each meeting, to verify that it was presented.

The purpose of the status report — like that of many other STEPS: Reports — is to keep management informed. An effective project status report should therefore include the following information:

CHECK
LIST

✔ Project identification

✔ The project's current status

✔ Areas of concern

✔ Items requiring action

By providing a regular reporting vehicle on the progress of the project, and by insisting on sign-off, you create ongoing contact with the user group managers. Keeping them involved in this way reduces exposure to risk, for both the project team and management.

# Project Status
# Report

Project ID: 930001-00

Project Name: N.Y. Sales Office LAN

Client Name: Sales Dept.

Project Leader: Bob Myers

Ref ID: PSR - 9301010001

Originator Name (Print): Bob Myers

Signature:

Date Completed:93/08/20

## *Accomplished This Period*

Finished cabling floors 1 to 3. Terminating jacks and wall outlets are completed.

## *Unresolved Problems Or Obstacles*

No problems to report this week.

## *Objectives For Next Period*

Finish cabling floor 4 and 5.

*Status Update - For Period Ending: (YY/MM/DD):*          93/08/20

| Task ID | Task Name | Start Date | % Complete | Est. Date for Completion | Notes |
|---------|-----------|-----------|-----------|--------------------------|-------|
| 001 | Install Cabling | 93/08/1 | 50% | 93/08/30 | Don't expect any problems |
|  |  |  |  |  |  |
|  |  |  |  |  |  |
|  |  |  |  |  |  |
|  |  |  |  |  |  |

## *Figure 8.3: Project Status Report*

### CHANGE AUTHORIZATION FORM

Though the project plan has now been approved, you can almost certainly anticipate requests to change items which have been agreed upon or are contract-related. Whether such changes originate with site management or with vendors, they are likely to represent additional costs and delays for the implementation.

It is essential for every change to be documented on a **change authorization form** like the one in Figure 8.4. The anticipated effects and costs of each change must be stated on the form. It is then presented to the project leader and the prime user group co-ordinator for approval. If a change affects the scope, cost, or work schedule of the project, the next step is to amend any related contract, so that it also reflects the change.

## A.5 Project Start-up Announcement

The project start-up announcement involves two tasks: distributing the approved project plan, and issuing the site communication memo.

### A.5.1 Distributing the Approved Project Plan

Once the appropriate authorizations have been obtained, the project leader distributes the approved project plan and a project start-up sign-off memo to the technology advisor and the prime user group co-ordinator for reference. Each team member also receives a copy of the project plan.

### A.5.2 Issuing the Site Communication Memo

With formal approvals in place, the project leader issues a site communication memo to the prime user group co-ordinator announcing project plan approval. In this memo, the project leader also formally requests a planned site visit.

The memo goes on to state both the main objectives of the visit and its agenda. The objectives are to inform management about what the project involves, and to set the stage for further investigative work by the project team. The latter measure is necessary to orient the users and to ensure that the team has enough data to develop the final system solution. The agenda for the visit typically includes the introduction of the project team, and a non-technical overview of the project by the project leader.

# Change Authorization Form

Ref. ID: CA - 9301010002_____

Request From:__Leslie Shvemar_____

Department:__3B11 - Cable Engineering_____

Requestor Signature:_____

Signing Authority:_____

## Change Request

| Ref. # | Description |
|--------|-------------|
| 001 | Change planned configuration of cable in building sector 7 (See attached recomm.plan) |
| | |
| | |
| | |
| | |
| | |
| | |
| | |
| | |

☐ Change Confirmed          ☑ Change Not Confirmed

Signature:_____          Date:_____

## Notes

| Re: Ref. # | Note |
|------------|------|
| 001 | Last minute office relocations. Cable spans too long. Will cause transmission problems. |
| | Recommend switching to cable type 1 and using alternate cable route 24 instead of route 25. |
| | |
| | |
| | |

*Figure 8.4: Change Authorization Form*

## B. TECHNICAL REQUIREMENTS AND DESIGN

The second activity in Phase I is establishing the technical requirements and design for the implementation. The project team combines the information from the needs analysis study with the findings from a complete physical — that is, technical — review of the environment. To complete this investigation, the team walks through and inspects the site. All the relevant information must be assembled before an appropriate solution can be developed. The STEPS: Forms are very useful here, since they are designed to organize and document all information requirements for later use.

Once the necessary material has been collected, the project team can produce the site inspection report, the first key deliverable in Phase I. An appropriate solution can now be developed and proposed for approval. This solution, also prepared by the project team, is documented in the system solution report, the second key deliverable in Phase I. However, the SSR contains more than just the system design for your LAN; it also documents the strategic operational plans necessary for the system's ongoing operation and maintenance.

You can see from Figure 8.5 that technical requirements and design involves six procedures: site visit preparation, management orientation and initial planning, physical site inspection, applications set-up, developing the solution, and developing the strategic operational plans. Each is examined in depth below.

### B.1 Site Visit Preparation

To prepare for the project team's site visit, two tasks must be completed: confirming the site visit dates, and preparing the site visit tools.

#### B.1.1 Confirming the Site Visit Dates

The technology advisor follows up the site communication memo (issued as part of the project start-up announcement) by confirming the dates on which the project team may conduct site planning and physical site inspection visits. The planning sessions are used to introduce management and key users to the implementation process and the material still to be gathered. For the site inspection, the technology advisor completes the skeleton diagrams for furniture and floor layout, while a cable specialist assesses the existing cabling environment.

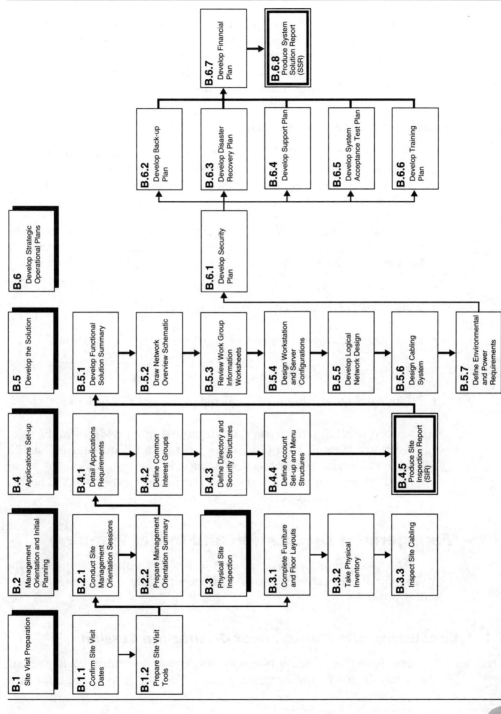

*Figure 8.5: STEPS: Process Chart for Phase I, Activity B — Technical Requirements and Design*

Normally, site planning and inspection take place concurrently over several days. For the purpose of this discussion, they will be dealt with in the order in which they would occur, should they have to be undertaken sequentially. The time required for the visits depends on the size of the project and the team resources available.

### B.1.2 Preparing the Site Visit Tools

Once the dates for the visits have been confirmed, the project team prepares all the necessary tools. These are used mainly by the technology advisor, for documenting all findings in a consistent fashion. The following tools are commonly used:

- All STEPS: Forms needed for management orientation and initial planning. The preparatory work of transferring some key components of the needs analysis to the appropriate worksheets must be done at this point.

- All STEPS: Forms needed for the physical site inspection

- Diagrams showing furniture and floor plans

- Existing wiring diagrams

- Technical tools and test gear required for taking measurements, etc.

For reasons of clarity, these tools are discussed in more detail in the relevant sections: Management Orientation and Initial Planning (section B.2 below), and Physical Site Inspection (section B.3 on page 137).

For a complete list of all forms and worksheets to be collected at this point, refer to Appendix B.

## B.2 Management Orientation and Initial Planning

Two tasks are to be accomplished in this procedure: conducting site management orientation sessions, and preparing the management orientation summary.

### B.2.1 Conducting Site Management Orientation Sessions

One objective of these planning sessions is to inform management about the details of the implementation. Another is to arrange for any additional investigative work that may be required, such as a review of existing material or the completion of outstanding details. While the initial management orientation session takes place at this point in the STEPS process, the meetings will continue over an extended period.

The STEPS: Forms listed below are discussed at the initial orientation session as those which will have to be reviewed or addressed in later planning meetings. You should be aware that, while these worksheets are discussed throughout this chapter as though they were sequential, in practice, they are often completed concurrently. They are not interdependent unless specified. For reasons of clarity, all the forms are discussed in detail elsewhere, as indicated.

- End user profile worksheets: These have already been completed by the users during needs analysis, but require review and updating. Chapter 2 provides more detail and a sample worksheet.

- Work group information worksheets: These are to be filled in at various points. Their use is discussed under tasks B.3.2, taking physical inventory (page 138); B.4.1, detailing applications requirements (page 145); B.4.2, defining common interest groups (page 149); and B.5.3, reviewing the work group information worksheets (page 161). A sample of this type of worksheet is shown on page 139.

- Applications details worksheets: These determine the nature of both the off-the-shelf and the customized applications presently used in the environment. More detail on these two-page worksheets follows under task B.4.1, detailing applications requirements, together with an illustration of each page (pages 145 - 47).

- Directory planning worksheets: These two-page worksheets define the basic workstation and server directory structures at the user, group, and organizational levels. They are discussed in detail and illustrated under task B.4.3, defining directory and security structures (pages 149 - 54).

- Security profile worksheets: These are used to map out the access requirements of the end users. They are also discussed in depth and illustrated under task B.4.3, defining directory and security structures (pages 149 - 54).

- Account set-up worksheets: These worksheets define default log-in parameters and account-related information for each end user. They are examined and illustrated under task B.4.4, defining account set-up and menu structures (pages 154 - 58).

- Menu options worksheets: These worksheets show menu structures. They are also discussed and illustrated under task B.4.4, defining account set-up and menu structures (pages 154 - 58).

At this point, the project team must take the functional requirements specification document (developed during needs analysis) one step farther, confirming that all the information necessary for completing the solution design will be made available. This is an important task, since the earlier research is focused on business needs and normally does not provide sufficient technical detail to develop the design.

This part of the STEPS process also offers a safety net in situations where the functional requirements specification document has not yet been developed, or must be altered. The latter might occur if corporate standards change, or if considerable time passes between the completion of the document and the next stage of the project.

Since the project team is introduced here, this is a good point at which to select the LAN administrator. This individual is designated by user group management, and needs to be familiar with both the business environment and the existing computer set-up. Depending on the scale of the implementation, there may be more than one LAN administrator. More information about the skill sets and responsibilities associated with this position can be found in Chapter 3. The LAN administrator will be closely involved in the completion of other tasks associated with the technical requirements and design portion of Phase I.

## B.2.2    Preparing the Management Orientation Summary

Once the management orientation sessions are over, the technology advisor writes an executive summary of the meetings. This document should focus on additions or changes to the information provided in the forms under review. Other items may be included as well:

- Issues or concerns regarding the upcoming site installation which the prime user group co-ordinator wishes to flag, e.g., possible disruption to important business needs such as inventory or year-end operations

- The assignment of the LAN administrator

- General training and system availability requirements

- How and when applications opportunities will be assessed

The summary is approved by the project leader and prime user group co-ordinator before being sent back to site management and, if appropriate, to corporate information systems management.

## B.3    Physical Site Inspection

The three tasks involved in the physical site inspection are completing furniture and floor layouts, taking physical inventory, and inspecting site cabling.

### B.3.1    *Completing Furniture and Floor Layouts*

This task is carried out whether the project involves the upgrade of an existing site or an entirely new building. In the latter case, the technology advisor must rely on architectural drawings and other building plans. A walk-through of the site should be done as soon as physically possible, to verify the information in the plans. No final system design can be completed without it.

The technology advisor fills in the details of the skeleton furniture and floor layout diagrams at the installation site, working together with a trained LAN installation specialist and a cable technician. The latter individuals are most often outside contractors. The completed floor layout diagrams should show the following items:

CHECK
LIST

✔ Existing and proposed furniture

✔ Existing and proposed computers and peripheral equipment

✔ Locations of electrical and communications (wiring) closets

✔ Locations and types of power and telecommunications receptacles and connectors (e.g., parallel, serial, RS232, etc.)

✔ Locations of conduit

✔ Locations of heating and air conditioning facilities

✔ Locations of wall partitions

✔ Locations of vertical risers (if this information is available)

This task is not to be overlooked. Omitting it can have dire consequences: In a recent implementation in a new building, the project team failed to confirm the physical details of the site. Just one week before the organization's scheduled move, the team discovered that four floors of the building had no conduit. Without conduit, wiring could not be properly fed to the workstations and telephones on those floors!

### B.3.2    *Taking Physical Inventory*

In taking physical inventory, the technology advisor records both hardware and software specifics for each workstation, server, and printer at the site. The technology advisor may be able to use a special software utility to scan the system and report on its configuration. A less preferred alternative is for the technology advisor or another party to undertake a physical inspection of each workstation, removing the cover and examining the hardware contents and settings.

Whichever approach is taken, the technology advisor must account for the existing base of PCs, servers, and printers, and the associated software. The main purpose of each workstation, the main software packages loaded on it, and whether the stations are presently standalone or networked must also be recorded. Three worksheets are used to document this information: the work group information worksheet, shown in Figure 8.6; the workstation configuration worksheet, shown in Figure 8.7; and the server configuration worksheet, shown in Figure 8.8.

This is the point at which the **work group information worksheet** is first used. This form gives a high-level view of all equipment and configurations within a given work group, looking at such details as type of PC, overall disk capacity, type of printer, and so on. The **workstation configuration worksheet** documents the "nuts and bolts" of the equipment, looking at such internal details as the type, number, and capacity of disk drives for each machine. The **server configuration worksheet** records details about the servers, including type of processor, type of disk storage, memory, and interfaces. Once all this information has been collected, the **equipment summary worksheet** (Figure 8.9) is filled in, providing a summary of equipment inventory. The information on all four worksheets will be used in developing the system solution.

# Work Group Information Worksheet

Ref ID: WI - 9301010001
Originator Name (Print): Ann Bigcanoe
Signature:
Date Completed:93/08/17

User Group: Accounts Payable  
Function: Data Entry  
Supervisor Name: Matt McCarthy  
Phone #: 111-222-3333

Department Name: Finance  
Dept. #/Location: 1234/2A

## Workstations and Servers

| System Type | Serial Number | Location | Hard Disk Capacity(Mb) | FDD | Total Memory | Monitor Type | Port ID | Cable Connection | Cable Type | Attached Printer Ser.# | Modem | Main Applications Loaded |
|---|---|---|---|---|---|---|---|---|---|---|---|---|
| PC486/33 | SN000000002 SN00000002 | 2B1 | 470 | 3.5.5.2 | 8Mb | VGA | 1 | 1CCT001 | UTP | SN111112 SN11111 | SYN19.2 | AcctPayXX.YYY, Inventry.YYY |
| PC386/25 | SN0000000000 | 2A10 | 150 | 3.5.5.2 | 4Mb | VGA | 2 | 1CCT002 | UTP | None | ASYN240 | App1, App2, App3... |
| PC386/25 | SN0000000000 | 2A11 | 150 | 3.5.5.2 | 4Mb | VGA | 3 | 1CCT003 | UTP | None | None | App1, App2, App3... |
| PC386/25 | SN0000000000 | 2A12 | 150 | 3.5.5.2 | 4Mbu | VGA | 4 | 1CCT004 | UTP | None | None | App1, App2, App3... |
|  |  |  |  |  |  |  |  |  |  |  |  |  |
|  |  |  |  |  |  |  |  |  |  |  |  |  |

## Printers

| Printer Type | Name/Model | Emulation(s) | Serial # | Shared /Ntwk | No. of Users | Memory (Mb) | No. Trays | Tray Types |
|---|---|---|---|---|---|---|---|---|
| Postscript | BrandXModelB |  | SN1111123 | ✓ | 3 | 4 | 2 | Letter, Legal |
| Serial Standard | BrandXModelA |  | SN11111 | ✓ | 3 |  | 0 | Continuous Feed Only |
|  |  |  |  |  |  |  |  |  |
|  |  |  |  |  |  |  |  |  |

## Interest Group(s)

| Dept. Name | Group Name | Location |
|---|---|---|
| Finance | Acc. Receiv. | 2C |
| Finance | Payments | 2D |
| Sales | Major Accts. | 5A |
| Sales | Gen. Accts. | 5B |

Figure 8.6: Work Group Information Worksheet

# Workstation Configuration Worksheet

Ref ID: SVR - _____9301010001_____

Originator Name (Print):___Raffi Anwar___

Signature:_____

Date Completed:_____94/07/07_____

## Processor and Bus Type

- [ ] 80286 _____
- [✓] 80386 DX/33
- [ ] 80486 _____
- [ ] Other:_____

- [✓] ISA
- [ ] EISA
- [ ] MCA
- [ ] Other:_____  Serial Number:___SN00000000000___

## Disk Storage Devices

- [ ] Floppy (1.2m 5.25In)
- [✓] Hard Drive 1 150 Mb    Space Left -1 __75Mb__
- [✓] Floppy (1.44m 3.5In)
- [ ] Hard Drive 2    Space Left -2_____

- [ ] Floppy (360kb 5.25In)
- [ ] Floppy (720Kb 3.5In)

Drive Type

- [ ] IDE
- [ ] MFM
- [✓] ESDI
- [ ] RRL
- [ ] Other:_____

## Memory

- [✓] Base RAM Size_640K_
- [✓] Extended____3Mb____
- [ ] Expanded_____

## Interfaces

- [✓] Serial __2__
- [✓] Parallel__1__
- [ ] SCSI_____
- [ ] Other:_____

## Graphics Card/Monitor Type

- [✓] VGA Color
- [ ] SVGA _____
- [ ] Other:_____   Resolution 640 X 480

- [ ] Interlaced
- [✓] Non-interlaced

## Network Interface Card

- [ ] 8 Bit
- [✓] 16 Bit
- [ ] 32 Bit

- [ ] Token Ring 4Mb
- [ ] Token Ring 16Mb
- [ ] Arcnet
- [✓] Ethernet
- [ ] Other:_____

Base Address____C000____   DMA____3____   Node Address _2_   IRQ____3____

## UPS

- [✓] Installed
- [ ] Not Installed

- [ ] 550VA
- [✓] 1000VA
- [ ] 1500V
- [ ] Other:_____

## Warranty

Vendor:_ABC Computers Inc._       Expiry Date:____94/12/31____

*Figure 8.7: Workstation Configuration Worksheet*

# Server Configuration Worksheet

Ref ID: SVR - _____ 93010001 _____
Originator Name (Print): _____ Dan Grant _____
Signature: _____
Date Completed: _____ 94/07/07 _____

## Processor and Bus Type

☐ 80286 ___  ☐ 80386 ___  ☑ 80486 DX33  ☐ Other: _____

☑ ISA  ☐ EISA  ☐ MCA  ☐ Other: _____  Serial Number: ___ SN000000002 _____

## Disk Storage Devices

☑ Floppy (1.2m 5.25In)   ☑ Hard Drive 1 500Mb   Space Left -1 300Mb   ☑ Mirror  ☑ Duplexed

☑ Floppy (1.44m 3.5In)   ☑ Hard Drive 2 _____   Space Left -2 _____   ☐ Mirror  ☐ Duplexed

☐ Floppy (360kb 5.25In)                          Drive Type

☐ Floppy (720Kb 3.5In)   ☐ IDE   ☐ MFM   ☑ ESDI   ☐ RRL   ☐ Other: _____

## Memory

☑ Base RAM Size 640K

☑ Extended 7Mb   ☑ Expanded _____

## Interfaces

☑ Serial 3   ☑ Parallel 3   ☐ SCSI _____   ☐ Other: _____

## Graphics Card/Monitor Type

☑ VGA Color   ☐ SVGA _____   ☐ Other: _____   Resolution 1024 X 768   ☑ Interlaced  ☐ Non-interlaced

## Network Interface Card

☐ 8 Bit   ☑ 16 Bit   ☐ 32 Bit

☐ Token Ring 4Mb   ☐ Token Ring 16Mb   ☐ Arcnet   ☑ Ethernet   ☐ Other: _____

Base Address C000   DMA 3   Node Address 2   IRQ 3

## UPS

☑ Installed   ☐ Not Installed

☐ 550VA   ☐ 1000VA   ☑ 1500V   ☐ Other: _____

## Warranty

Vendor: ABC Computers Inc.   Expiry Date: 94/12/31

*Figure 8.8: Server Configuration Worksheet*

# Equipment Summary
# Worksheet

Ref ID: EQS - 9301010001

Originator Name (Print): Norm Saunders

Signature:

Date Completed:93/08/17

## Checklist of Equipment

### Computers

| Model Name | CPU Type | Monitor Name | Monitor Type | Count |
|---|---|---|---|---|
| ABC 486XL | 486DX/33 | ABCTrue Screen | VGA | 1 |
| ABC 386EL | 386SX/25 | ABCTrue Screen | VGA | 3 |
| | | | | |
| | | | | |
| | | | | |
| | | | | |

### Printers

| Model Name | Printer Type | Postscript | Compatibility List | Count |
|---|---|---|---|---|
| BrandXModelA | Serial Standard Matrix | | | 1 |
| BrandXModelB | Laser | ✓ | HGII, HGIII | 2 |
| | | | | |
| | | | | |
| | | | | |
| | | | | |

Has the site been cabled: ☐ Yes ☑ No

### Comments

*Figure 8.9: Equipment Summary Worksheet*

### B.3.3　*Inspecting Site Cabling*

The cable technician examines the wiring closets, then completes the **wiring closet information worksheet** (Figure 8.10). During this exercise, the types and locations of cables, horizontal conduits, and vertical risers are examined, and the locations either noted or verified on the furniture and floor layout diagrams.

The **cable information worksheet** (Figure 8.11) is also completed at this time. It accounts for all existing cable terminations.

The worksheets and diagrams together provide the technical design team with a snapshot of the existing site cabling system and equipment topography. This information is essential for determining the cabling system and connectivity requirements or upgrades for the new LAN.

## B.4　Applications Set-up

The applications set-up procedure consists of five tasks: detailing the applications requirements, defining common interest groups, defining directory and security structures, defining account set-up and menu structures, and producing the site inspection report.

### B.4.1　*Detailing Applications Requirements*

The technology advisor is responsible for completing the **applications details worksheets**. This time-consuming task is usually accomplished with the help of the LAN administrator and other site staff.

The applications details worksheets establish the nature of the commercially available and the custom-developed applications currently used in the environment. An example of this type of two-page worksheet appears in Figure 8.12.

On the worksheet, each application is categorized as a LAN/network or a standalone version. A network version application is licensed and/or capable of being shared among many users. A standalone version application is intended for a single user only. This information is needed to determine the actual and anticipated support needs of the system solution. Special considerations regarding the various applications are noted under the heading "Special Set-up Instructions" on worksheet. The following are some special parameters within the applications environment that require customization:

- HP PCL, postscript or standard printing, duplex printing

# Wiring Closet Information Worksheet

Ref ID: WC - 9301010001

**CLOSET ID/LOCATION** Floor 3 North East Wall

Originator Name (Print): Brian Collie

Signature:

Date Completed:93/08/17

## Existing

☐ Type I        Note _____

☐ Type II        _____

☑ Unshielded Twisted Pair    _____

☐ Other_____    _____

Site Name: XYZ Manufacturing NY Sales

Installer: Hannah Oatley

## Environmental Specifications

Closet Dimensions    Length  3 m        Width  3 m        Height  3.7 m

Number of Receptacles: 5

Number of Shelves: 10

Ambient Closet Temperature: 23        Degrees ☑ Centigrade  ☐ Fahrenheit

Ventilation    ☑ Fan        ☐ Ventilation Slots

## Notes

Building only 2 years old. Closets set up for UTP cable. Other LANs present in building. Clean throughout. Door is not secure.
- Recommend door replacement with steel door.
- Already wired with Unshielded Twisted Pair

*Figure 8.10: Wiring Closet Information Worksheet*

# Cable Information Worksheet

☐ Type I

☐ Type II

☑ Unshielded Twisted Pair   UTP Throughout

☐ Other:_____   _____

Notes: _____

_____

Ref ID: CAB - 9301010001_____

Originator Name(Print): Josh Levine_____

Signature:_____

Date Completed:93/08/14_____

Site Name: XYZ Manufacturing Inc. New York Sales

## Cabling Checklist

| Cable/Port ID | User Name | Office Location | Passed(Y/N) | Power |
|---|---|---|---|---|
| 1CCT002/2 | Lauren Thompson | 2A10 | ✓ | ✓ |
| 1CCT003/3 | Sarah Nadas | 2A11 | ✓ | ✓ |
| 1CCT004/4 | Teanning Chung | 2A12 | ✓ | ✓ |
| 1CCT001/1 | No User - Work Group Server | 2B1 | ✓ | ✓ |
| | | | | |
| | | | | |
| | | | | |
| | | | | |
| | | | | |
| | | | | |
| | | | | |
| | | | | |
| | | | | |
| | | | | |
| | | | | |
| | | | | |
| | | | | |
| | | | | |
| | | | | |

Note: For cabling to pass, it must have all the end connectors attached and must be fully functional. For power to pass, there must be a power receptacle present at each desk. It must be capable of handling the anticipated electrical load.

*Figure 8.11: Cable Information Worksheet*

# Applications Details Worksheet
## - Commercial -

Ref ID: APP - _9301010001_

Originator Name (Print): _Choi Wai Luon_

Signature:_____

Date Completed:_93/08/07_

*Commercial Applications*

| Application Name | Version | LAN Version | # of Nodes | Size (Mb) | Main Use |
|---|---|---|---|---|---|
| WordProcess | 5.1 | ✓ | 25 | 2 | Word Processing - correspondence |
| | | | | | |
| | | | | | |
| | | | | | |
| | | | | | |
| | | | | | |
| | | | | | |
| | | | | | |
| | | | | | |
| | | | | | |
| | | | | | |
| | | | | | |
| | | | | | |

*Special Set-up Instructions*

| Application Name | Instructions |
|---|---|
| | |
| | |
| | |
| | |
| | |
| | |
| | |

*Figure 8.12: Applications Details Worksheet (Commercial)*

# Applications Details Worksheet
## - Custom -

Ref ID: APP - 9301010001

Originator Name (Print): Choi Wai Luon

Signature:

Date Completed: 93/08/07

*Custom Applications*

| Application Name | Version | LAN Version | # of Nodes | Size (Mb) | Main Use |
|---|---|---|---|---|---|
| AcctPayXX.YYY | 1.0 | ✓ | 25 | 2 | Data Entry For Payables |
| Inventry.YYY | 3 | ✓ | 5 | 1 | Inventory Master |
| | | | | | |
| | | | | | |
| | | | | | |
| | | | | | |
| | | | | | |
| | | | | | |
| | | | | | |
| | | | | | |
| | | | | | |
| | | | | | |
| | | | | | |
| | | | | | |

*Special Set-up Instructions*

| Application Name | Instructions |
|---|---|
| AcctPayXX.YYY | Make Sure Buffers are set to at least 32 in Config.Sys |
| | |
| | |
| | |
| | |
| | |

*Figure 8.12, cont'd.: Applications Details Worksheet (Custom)*

- Special video display adaptor requirements

- Microsoft Windows environment, memory requirements

- E-mail access

Once all relevant information has been compiled on the applications details worksheet, it is summarized in the **network applications summary worksheet**, shown in Figure 8.13.

At this time, all software change requirements are noted on the work group information worksheet. The identity and software needs of individuals or groups that are not presently automated and have not been included on the same worksheet are also noted. Information about hardware may be added during the next procedure, developing the solution (B.5).

### B.4.2    *Defining Common Interest Groups*

This task is done to ensure that all details about the functional needs of the end users are considered at the design stage. During needs analysis, each work group identified its own information-sharing patterns and requirements. The technology advisor entered this material under the heading "Interest Group" on the work group information worksheets during preparation for the site visit. Now the worksheets are completed, with the addition of the remaining information about the users' needs.

At this point, the work group information worksheets contain up-to-date information about individual work groups' applications needs and about common interest groups. For instance, the worksheets may reflect the actual or anticipated need of your marketing group to access and work directly with data on sales and inventory. The information on the worksheets must be complete, so that directory structures and security profiles may be properly defined.

### B.4.3    *Defining Directory and Security Structures*

This task is somewhat technical in nature. It requires all the completed worksheets from the tasks done thus far in this procedure, together with an understanding of system directories and security structures. The technology advisor is therefore responsible for completing it.

The technology advisor uses the **directory planning worksheet** to define the directory structures of both workstations and servers at the user, group, and organizational levels. Figure 8.14 shows an example of the two-page directory planning worksheet. Existing directory structure

# Network
# Applications Summary
# Worksheet

Ref ID: NAPP - 9301010001

## Summary

| Item | Summary Description |
|---|---|
| AcctPayXX.YY | Main Accounts Payable System. Used By All AP Clerks |
| WordProcess | Standard Word Processor |
| Inventry.YYY | Inventory System |
|  |  |
|  |  |
|  |  |
|  |  |
|  |  |

## Applications Loaded

| Applications Loaded | Version # | Network Version | User/Group(s) |
|---|---|---|---|
| AcctPayXX.YYY | 1.0 | ✓ | Accounts Payable, Accounting |
| WordProcess | 5.1 | ✓ | All |
| Inventry.YYY | 2.1 | ✓ | Finance |
|  |  |  |  |
|  |  |  |  |
|  |  |  |  |
|  |  |  |  |
|  |  |  |  |

Completed By: Aris Economopolis          On Date: 93/08/17

*Figure 8.13: Network Applications Summary Worksheet*

# Directory Planning Worksheet

User Name/ID:  Jean Paul Lauzon/JPLAUZON

Group Name/ID:  Accounts Payable/AP

Organization Name/ID:  Finance/FIN

Ref ID: DP -  9301010001

Originator Name (Print):  Eli Grimson

Signature:

Date Completed: 93/08/16

## Root Directory

| Directory Name | WP | SPREADS | INVOICES | INVENTRY | BANKREC | ACCOUNT |
|---|---|---|---|---|---|---|
| Reference # | D1 | D2 | D3 | D4 | D5 | D6 |

| Directory Name | APSOFTW | | | | | |
|---|---|---|---|---|---|---|
| Reference # | D7 | | | | | |

| Directory Name | | | | | | |
|---|---|---|---|---|---|---|
| Reference # | | | | | | |

| Directory Name | | | | | | |
|---|---|---|---|---|---|---|
| Reference # | | | | | | |

| Directory Name | | | | | | |
|---|---|---|---|---|---|---|
| Reference # | | | | | | |

| Directory Name | | | | | | |
|---|---|---|---|---|---|---|
| Reference # | | | | | | |

| Directory Name | | | | | | |
|---|---|---|---|---|---|---|
| Reference # | | | | | | |

*Figure 8.14: Directory Planning Worksheet*

# Directory Planning Worksheet

User Name/ID: Jean Paul Lauzon/JPLAUZON

Group Name/ID: Accounts Payable/AP

Organization Name/ID: Finance/FIN

Ref ID: DP - 9301010001

Originator Name (Print): Eli Grimson

Signature:

Date Completed:93/08/16

*Reference #:* D1

## Sub-Directories

| Sub-Directory | CORRESP | PERSNNL | ADMIN | FORMLTR | | |
|---|---|---|---|---|---|---|
| Reference # | D1/1 | D1/2 | D1/3 | D1/4 | | |
| Sub-Directory | | | | | | |
| Reference # | | | | | | |
| Sub-Directory | | | | | | |
| Reference # | | | | | | |
| Sub-Directory | | | | | | |
| Reference # | | | | | | |
| Sub-Directory | | | | | | |
| Reference # | | | | | | |
| Sub-Directory | | | | | | |
| Reference # | | | | | | |
| Sub-Directory | | | | | | |
| Reference # | | | | | | |

*Figure 8.14: Directory Planning Worksheet (continued)*

guidelines established by the organization must be followed when completing the worksheet. Any deviations in directory structures from organizational standards require the project leader's approval. The technology advisor must complete the worksheet before defining security structures.

The paragraphs below provide some background about directory and security structures, to help you understand what is involved in defining them.

Directories provide storage locations for subdirectories, also known as files, on a workstation's or server's hard disk. The difference between the latter is that a workstation is a standalone set-up, while a server is part of a network. Each file is given a name, organized hierarchically — much like in a traditional filing cabinet — and stored at a specific location so it can be found quickly. The various directory levels in the structure can be thought of as corresponding to the filing cabinet, a file drawer, the hanging folders within the drawer, and the manilla envelopes within each folder that contain the files.

An important point about directory structures is that the terms "directory" and "subdirectory" are always relative. A given directory is a subdirectory in relation to the directory above it in the hierarchy. At the same time, it is a parent directory to the one below it. You can see an example of a DOS-based directory structure in Figure 8.15.

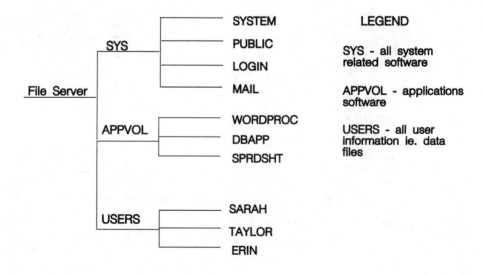

*Figure 8.15: Sample DOS-based Directory Structure*

A security structure is best explained as a means of controlling access — defining access privileges — to information stored in various directories and files. Security structures include the following:

- Log-in security:  Who can access the workstation or network

- Rights security:  Which directories and files a specific user or user group may access

- Attribute security:  What users can do with the directories and files accessible to them

Developing effective security structures is a vital part of your implementation. This is true regardless of the size of your LAN, since its introduction may place vital information about such sensitive matters as the organization's financial status or personnel files in a shared domain.

A filtering system known as a **rights mask** may be used to define access privileges for information resources ranging from computer programs to databases. The rights mask acts as a locking mechanism, either allowing or barring access to information on an individual, group, and organizational level. It also controls the ability to execute specific procedures. As an example, suppose that Taylor Maavara may be happy to share her documented inventory reports for viewing purposes, but does not want anyone to be able to change them. On the other hand, she works closely with the accounting department. Therefore, rather than having them review her books in printed form, she may find it useful to allow the accounting personnel more access so that they may reconcile her bank statements with live data. Table 8.1 shows examples of common rights masks.

Rights masks are established by the technology advisor and the LAN administrator, on the basis of information in the functional requirements specification document, notes from management orientation sessions, and both the work group information worksheets and directory planning worksheets. First, directory access is determined for each group and user. Then the directory names and rights masks are assigned on the **security profile worksheets**. (Figure 8.16 shows a security profile worksheet.) It is in this way that access privileges are assigned to other users and interest groups. Because of the vital importance of information security in LANs, each security profile worksheet must be signed by its information owner. The security profile worksheets must conform to any existing corporate information security plan. The information they contain forms a critical component of the LAN security plan, which is developed later in Phase I.

| Rights Mask | | Description |
|---|---|---|
| R | Read Only | Look at specific information |
| W | Write Only | Add/replace information in a file |
| O | Open File | Access information to read or write |
| C | Create | Create new files in a specific directory |
| D | Delete | Remove files |
| S | Search | Conduct a search of stored data |
| P | Parental | Create directories |
| M | Modify | Alter existing files |

*Table 8.1: Some Common Rights Masks*

### B.4.4   *Defining Account Set-up and Menu Structures*

The technology advisor defines the account set-up by specifying the default log-in parameters for each user account. These parameters have to do with the allocation of disk space, the length of passwords, permitted log-in access times, account expiry dates, and so on. The account set-up also controls the ability of others to log in to specific accounts, as established by the rights masks. Typically, a standard set of log-in parameters is used for an entire user group. The parameters may be changed as needed by the LAN administrator.

The technology advisor completes the **account set-up worksheets**, filling in the user's, group's, or organization's name; account expiry dates; and the applications access section. The account set-up worksheet is shown in Figure 8.17.

Before you read about defining menu structures, you may find some background information useful. Menu structure refers to the set of menu screens with which a user accesses applications, as well as to the order in which the screens appear. The flow of the menu structure is typically

# Security Profile Worksheet

Ref ID: SEC - 9301010001

Originator Name (Print):Gian Brandolisio

Signature:

Date Completed:93/08/17

Owner Name

User Name: Lauren Eden

Group Name:

Organization Name: H.Q. Marketing

Owner Signature:

Date:93/08/17

## Effective Rights

### Access Given To - Delegate Name

| Directory Path | User Name | Group Name | Organization Name | Access Rights | Notes |
|---|---|---|---|---|---|
| **C:\SAMPLE\DATA\paymaster** | | **H.Q. Finance** | | **RWOM** | **Needed For Month-End** |
| G:\FORECASTS | Scott Taylor | Forecasting | Finance | R | Data for revenue project'ns |
| G:\PRODINFO | | Major Accts | Sales | R | Product info for sales staff |
| G:\FEEDBACK | | Major Accts | Sales | RW | Sales feedback for mktg |
| G:\SFTWRE\CONFIGS | | | Sales | ROFX | Product Pricing Programs |
| | | | | | |
| | | | | | |
| | | | | | |
| | | | | | |
| | | | | | |
| | | | | | |
| | | | | | |
| | | | | | |
| | | | | | |
| | | | | | |
| | | | | | |
| | | | | | |
| | | | | | |
| | | | | | |
| | | | | | |

| | | |
|---|---|---|
| R=Read Only | D=Delete | E=Erase |
| W=Write Only | S=Search | F=File Scan |
| O=Open Only | P=Parental | A=Access Control |
| C=Create | M=Modify | X=Execute |

___ = ___
___ = ___
___ = ___
___ = ___

*Figure 8.16: Security Profile Worksheet*

# Account Set-up Worksheet

User Name/ID: Robert Quadrini /RQTOWNE

Group Name/ID: Accounts Payable/AP

Organization Name/ID: Finance/FIN

Electronic Mail ID: FIN/AP/RQTOWNE

Ref ID: ASW - 9301010001

Originator Name (Print): Choi Wai Luon

Signature:

Date Completed:93/08/14

## Default Settings

Date Account Expires(YY/MM/DD): **93/12/05**
Max. Connections:  2
Min. Password Length:  5
# Log-ins Allowed:  3
Max Disk Space (Mb):  150

Require Unique            ☑ Yes      ☐ No

Restrict Sign-on Between  12:00 am  to  12:00 pm   on  Sat, Sun          (Time=HH:MMam)
Restrict Sign-on Between  6:30 pm   to  8:00 am    on  Mon-Fri
Restrict Sign-on Between _____  to _____  on _____
Restrict Sign-on Between _____  to _____  on _____
Restrict Sign-on Between _____  to _____  on _____
Restrict Sign-on Between _____  to _____  on _____

## Application Access

| Application Name/Path | Read Only | Read/ Write | Write Only | Note |
|---|---|---|---|---|
| G:\FIN\ACCPAY\AcctPayXX.YYY | | ✓ | | Payables Clerk |
| F:\CORP\EMAIL | | ✓ | | Corporate Electronic Mail |
| | | | | |
| | | | | |
| | | | | |
| | | | | |
| | | | | |
| | | | | |
| | | | | |
| | | | | |
| | | | | |
| | | | | |

*Figure 8.17: Account Set-up Worksheet*

organized according to a hierarchy. Like other structures, menu structure may be defined and standardized at the individual, group, or organizational level.

Figure 8.18 illustrates a possible format for a main menu screen. The screen which follows this one will consist entirely of options relating to the user's first selection. For instance, if you choose Option 1 from the main menu screen, then different word processing options will appear. However, if you select Option 2, the next screen will offer various spreadsheet options, and so on.

| **Main Menu** | |
|---|---|
| 1 | Wordprocessing |
| 2 | Spreadsheets |
| 3 | Graphics Options |

*Figure 8.18 Sample Main Menu Screen*

Reviewing the existing menu structures is the task of the technology advisor and the LAN administrator. If new requirements need to be added, they adjust the information, then enter the results on the two-page **menu options worksheet** (Figure 8.19; only one page of this figure is illustrated since the second is simply a continuation used when additional space is required). While this information may not yet be final, it is important for both developing the solution later on in Phase I, and setting up user accounts on the network during pre-configuration and testing in Phase II.

## B.4.5 Milestone · *Producing the Site Inspection Report (SIR)*

The site inspection report is the first key deliverable of the STEPS process. Its completion is the fourth milestone in the process. The document provides details about the functional and physical aspects of the organization's present operating environment, gathered during the site planning meetings and the physical site inspection. This material falls into two distinct categories, one relating to the applications needs of the

# Menu Options Worksheet

User Name/ID: Francesca Santos/FSANTOS

Group Name/ID: Accounts Payable/AP

Organization Name/ID: Finance/FIN

Ref ID: MNU - 9301010001

Originator Name (Print): Gino Ruffo

Signature:

Date Completed: 93/08/17

## Main Menu

| Ref. # | Menu Items | Batch File To Execute |
|--------|------------|-----------------------|
| 001 | Accounts Payable | ACCXXX.YYY |
| 002 | Word Processing | WPXXX.ZZZ |
| 003 | Electronic Mail | EMXXX.ZZZ |
| 004 | Executive Calendar | CAXXX.ZZZ |
| | | |
| | | |
| | | |

*Sub-Menu:* 001

| Ref. # | Menu Items | Batch File To Execute |
|--------|------------|-----------------------|
| 001/1 | Accounts Payable Master File | APMFXX.ZZZ |
| 001/2 | Main Data Entry Module | DEMXX.ZZZ |
| 001/3 | Invoices | INVXX.ZZZ |
| | | |
| | | |
| | | |
| | | |

*Sub-Menu:*

| Ref. # | Menu Items | Batch File To Execute |
|--------|------------|-----------------------|
| | | |
| | | |
| | | |
| | | |
| | | |
| | | |

*Figure 8.19: Menu Options Worksheet*

158

users, and the other relating to the features of the physical site. It is important to recall here that, although the tasks involved in compiling the information have been discussed sequentially, many of them occur concurrently in practice. They are not interdependent unless specified.

The site inspection report contains completed worksheets and floor plans (all of which you have now seen examples of), bound in the following order:

CHECK
LIST

✔ Site management orientation sessions summary

✔ End user profile worksheets

✔ Work group information worksheets

✔ Directory planning worksheets (2 pages)

✔ Security profile worksheets

✔ Account set-up worksheets

✔ Menu options worksheets (2 pages)

✔ Applications details worksheets — commercial and custom (2 pages)

✔ Workstation configuration worksheets

✔ Server configuration worksheets

✔ Furniture and floor plans

✔ Equipment summary worksheets

✔ Cable information worksheets

✔ Wiring closet information worksheets

The number of worksheets actually bound in your site inspection report will vary with the size and complexity of your LAN. All two-page worksheets have been noted on the list, for your reference.

The SIR is packaged by the technology advisor for use in developing the system solution report, at the end of the technical requirements and design activity.

# B.5    Developing the Solution

Seven tasks are involved in the development of the system solution: developing the functional solution summary, drawing the network overview schematic, reviewing the work group information worksheets, designing workstation and server configurations, developing the logical network design, designing the cabling system, and defining environmental and power requirements. They are examined in turn below.

## B.5.1    *Developing the Functional Solution Summary*

The functional solution summary is an executive overview of the organization's business requirements, as laid out in the functional requirements specification document and the site inspection report. It summarizes the main network functions and key features that your system will require. The following information is included in the functional solution summary:

- Solution functions: The ability to share information and printing resources, access remote communications, and so on

- Solution features: E-mail, appointment scheduling, Windows environment, etc.

- Network applications: Names of the network software packages that may be used to provide the functions and features listed above

The next component of the functional solution summary is an itemized list of business applications which will reside in the LAN. The list includes both commercial and custom applications, as specified in the applications details worksheets. Some examples of such applications are accounting, word processing, and any other job that your organization or work group has decided should be done on a LAN. The applications are listed in the order of their relative importance. Also included in the summary are the user groups that correspond to the applications.

You may recall from Chapter 2 that, once the functional requirements specification document is finished, the project team is in a good position to develop and issue the  request for information and request for quotation. These documents provide additional input into the planning process. If they have not yet been issued, this is a good time. In practice, the documents may be issued at any point before the system solution report is finalized. The timing depends largely on the complexity of the LAN and the availability of resources.

### B.5.2    *Drawing the Network Overview Schematic*

The **network overview schematic** is a high-level blueprint of the proposed layout for the work environment. It provides a conceptual look at the types and locations of all major LAN components and their means of interconnection. The schematic is based on the information about furniture and floor layout in the site inspection report. A graphic view of the proposed network enhances this information. The drawing is accompanied by a written description of the networking software elements to be used in the environment — network operating systems, gateway products, and so on.

The network overview schematic illustrates the following features of the site:

CHECK
LIST

✔ Furniture and floor layouts

✔ Communications rooms

✔ The locations of conduit

✔ All computing devices, such as workstations, servers, and mainframes

✔ Internetwork devices, such as bridges, routers, and gateways

✔ Peripheral devices, such as printers

✔ Types of connections

✔ The means by which each device is to be connected to the network

### B.5.3    *Reviewing the Work Group Information Worksheets*

The next task is for the technology advisor to review and update the existing work group information worksheets and prepare additional worksheets for all new devices to be acquired for the implementation. The technology advisor then collates all the worksheets to produce a complete and accurate set providing a high-level view of all equipment. To do this exercise properly, the technology advisor must use highly technical references, including the completed applications details worksheets, and vendor- and/or product-specific computer and communications standards documentation. The reference material must be closely examined to verify conformity to standards and continuity. Any changes or clarifications related to the work group information worksheets must be cleared with the technology advisor.

Once all worksheets have been completed, the technology advisor delivers them, together with all references, to the project leader. The information will be used during Phases II and III of the STEPS process.

This careful, thorough approach to the task guarantees that all devices — existing and new — will be incorporated into the solution. It also highlights the requisite upgrades for existing devices, which will vary from site to site. The process of upgrading, whether during site preparation or LAN installation, is thereby simplified.

## B.5.4   *Designing Workstation and Server Configurations*

The configurations for all components of the proposed LAN, both existing and new, can now be carefully thought out and designed. Any upgrades to existing equipment, such as increased memory requirements, are now incorporated in the solution as well.

In the course of this task, the technology advisor reviews and updates the work group information, workstation configuration, server configuration, and equipment summary worksheets. The newly designed configuration information is entered on these worksheets, which are then collated. As in the previous task, the technology advisor must make use of technical references when doing this work, after ascertaining that they conform to standards and continuity. The finished material is delivered to the project leader. Again, this thorough-going approach ensures that both existing and new devices are incorporated into the system solution.

## B.5.5   *Developing the Logical Network Design*

The development of the logical network design is the point at which the operating environment of your LAN is tailored to your organization's needs. This design takes into account such matters as security, directory structures, menus, log-in parameters, and applications support. In short, it documents the software configuration and set-up as it applies to the organization.

By this time, all but one of the worksheets associated with Phase I has been completed. This is the two-page **operating system configuration**

**worksheet**, shown in Figure 8.20, which defines the parameters for the operating system. The operating system configuration worksheet is now filled in.

The logical network design package consists of the following worksheets:

CHECK
LIST

✔ Work group information worksheets

✔ Server configuration worksheets

✔ Workstation configuration worksheets

✔ Operating system configuration worksheets (2 pages)

✔ Account set-up worksheets

✔ Menu options worksheets (2 pages)

✔ Security profile worksheets

✔ Directory planning worksheets (2 pages)

✔ Applications details worksheets — commercial and custom (2 pages)

✔ Network applications summary worksheet

## B.5.6  *Designing the Cabling System*

The cabling diagrams are the core of the cabling system design. They are based on the furniture and floor layout diagrams prepared earlier for the site inspection report. The drawings indicate the types of connections at each cable end, as well as the types of cables along the various cable runs. The runs are shown travelling up or down risers and across floors via the communications rooms and conduits depicted in the network overview schematic. In short, the cabling diagrams provide the details about cabling which are not included in the network overview schematic.

The diagrams are accompanied by a written explanation of the design. The document also explains why the particular LAN topology and cabling scheme were chosen. New cable information worksheets are completed on the basis of the document, and packaged with the other up-to-date worksheets completed during site inspection. This information will be used by the cable installation specialist during Phase II.

# Operating System Configuration Worksheet

☑ Novell Netware    Version: _3.2_    Server Name: SERVER1        Ref ID: NOS - _9301010003_

☐ Banyan Vines            _____    Workstation ID: _____    Originator Name (Print): _Pascale Ashworth_

☐ Microsoft LAN Manager  _____    Network Address: 1_____    Signature: _____

☐ Other: _____       _____    Communications Buffers: _55_    Date Completed: 93/12/31

## Resource Sets

*Communications/LAN Interface Boards*

| LAN ID | Name/Description | Option # | Interrupt IRQ | I/O Base Address | DMA | Network Address |
|--------|-----------------|----------|---------------|------------------|-----|-----------------|
| A | ABCFastcardE-Net 32Bit | 1 | 2 | 2E0 | 2 | 1 |
| | | | | | | |
| | | | | | | |
| | | | | | | |
| | | | | | | |
| | | | | | | |

*Hard Disk Channel Drives*

| Chan # | Name/Description | Option # | Interrupt IRQ | I/O Base Address | DMA | Notes |
|--------|-----------------|----------|---------------|------------------|-----|-------|
| 1 | Quantum-X | 2 | 14 | 1F0 | | |
| | | | | | | |
| | | | | | | |
| | | | | | | |
| | | | | | | |
| | | | | | | |

Other: _____    Optical Disk Drive _____

| Ref. # | Name/Description | Option # | Interrupt IRQ | I/O Base Address | DMA | Notes |
|--------|-----------------|----------|---------------|------------------|-----|-------|
| 2 | OPTICOM-A | 0 | | D0001 | | Used For Clip Art |
| | | | | | | |
| | | | | | | |
| | | | | | | |
| | | | | | | |

*Figure 8.20: Operating System Configuration Worksheet*

# Operating System Configuration Worksheet

Ref ID: NOS - 9301010003

Originator Name (Print): Pascale Ashworth

Signature:_____

Date Completed:93/12/31

## Resource Sets

*Serial Printer Configurations*

| Port | Serial #/Name | Printer Type | Baud Rate | Word Size | Stop Bits | Parity | xon /xoff | Poll | Int | Queue Name | Spool # |
|------|---------------|--------------|-----------|-----------|-----------|--------|-----------|------|-----|------------|---------|
| 1 | SN111111/BrandXModel | Standard | 9600 | 7 | 7 | off | | 15 sec | 4 | PRN1 | 5 |
| | | | | | | | | | | | |
| | | | | | | | | | | | |
| | | | | | | | | | | | |
| | | | | | | | | | | | |

*Parallel Printer Configurations*

| Port | Serial #/Name | Printer Type | Poll | Interrupt | Queue Name | Spool # |
|------|---------------|--------------|------|-----------|------------|---------|
| 2 | SN11111123/BrandX-XA | Postscript | 15 sec | 7 | PRN2 | 4 |
| | | | | | | |
| | | | | | | |
| | | | | | | |
| | | | | | | |

*Volume Information*

| Volume Name | Directory Cached(Y/N) | # of Directory Entries | Size (Mb) | Notes |
|-------------|-----------------------|------------------------|-----------|-------|
| ACCVOL | No | 5 | 255 | Accounting Information |
| SYS 1 | Yes | 20 | 500 | Main |
| | | | | |
| | | | | |
| | | | | |
| | | | | |
| | | | | |

*Figure 8.20: Operating System Configuration Worksheet (continued)*

### B.5.7 *Defining Environmental and Power Requirements*

This task involves drawing a series of diagrams depicting environmental and power requirements. The drawings are based on the furniture and floor layout diagrams. In addition, they detail any unusual power and environmental requirements — special furniture, appliances, or electrical outlets; the condition of the air (e.g., dusty, dry, etc.); and unique architectural elements — which must be taken into consideration when accommodating the proposed solution. The diagrams are accompanied by a written account that includes any special features of the design.

This task may seem to be a fuss over minor details, particularly if the LAN is to be installed in a new building, since most designs provide for fairly standard power arrangements. However, it is important to keep in mind the fundamental value of STEPS: that by following the process thoroughly and systematically, you cover all custom details for your LAN.

## B.6 Developing the Strategic Operational Plans

In any LAN implementation, the tasks that must be handled are numerous and usually complex. The natural tendency for installers and administrators, therefore, is to address the many issues at hand and put aside those which do not appear to have immediate impact. Unfortunately, among the items most commonly set aside are the strategic operational plans. These plans are essential to the successful installation, operation, and ongoing management of your LAN. For this reason, they are developed and packaged as part of the proposed solution. Furthermore, all the strategic operational plans — except the system acceptance test plan — should be dynamic documents which are continually updated after implementation. Chapter 6 is devoted to strategic operational plans, because of their central importance.

The strategic operational plans are developed primarily by the technology advisor, with input from management. Keep in mind, however, that because of the nature and complexity of the work involved here, it might be wise to enlist some outside assistance. A little purchased expertise in the form of a consultant, contractor, or vendor can go a long way toward eliminating potential problems.

The sections that follow examine the strategic operational plans in the order in which they are presented in both Figure 8.5 (the process chart for the technical requirements and design activity) and Chapter 6: security plan, back-up plan, disaster recovery plan, support plan, system acceptance test plan, training plan, and financial plan. The final section deals with the task of producing the system solution report. If you feel the summaries of the various strategic operational plans are somewhat brief, remember that Chapter 6 offers a more in-depth treatment.

### B.6.1    Developing the Security Plan

One of the most critical areas in the operation of any LAN is security. Too little protection leaves the LAN vulnerable to intrusion, while too much security is seen by the users as intrusive. There are two general approaches to establishing LAN security: using the network operating system to establish access rights, and installing special security products such as data encryption devices. The decision as to what form of security your implementation requires, and how you can administer it, is examined in Chapter 6.

The security plan sets out the elements of your information security, instructions for its use, and the means of measuring its success. The completed security plan must be developed before any of the other strategic operational plans. Once completed, it must be approved by senior management, becoming corporate policy. Approval may be given before the security plan is included in the system solution report, or as part of the overall design approval.

### B.6.2    Developing the Back-up Plan

The purpose of the back-up plan is to create an organized, documented approach to avoiding the loss or corruption of data. The plan is intended to ensure that all information is copied on a regular basis and exists in duplicate. The back-up plan and the accompanying back-up log together serve as a documentation aid for the LAN administrator during full system operation.

As Chapter 6 pointed out, the back-up plan is generally presented in terms of periodic back-up cycles, time of day, and the media used. It is important to design the back-up strategy with both safety and convenience in mind. The safety factor guarantees that, in the event of problems with the system, you will always have available a very recent copy of all your data. The convenience aspect helps to ensure that back-ups do, in fact, take place.

The back-up plan is an important component of the next strategic operational plan to be developed, the disaster recovery plan.

### B.6.3    *Developing the Disaster Recovery Plan*

The disaster recovery plan is intended to protect against network-related failures beyond the organization's control, and perhaps even originating outside the building. Determining the extent of the coverage needed can be a difficult decision, possibly affecting both the structure and the cost of facilities inside and outside of the LAN site. Overprotection tends to be costly; on the other hand, underprotection can expose the organization's data.

The development of the disaster recovery plan is one of the tasks to consider handing over to an outside resource. Because of their experience in this area, third parties are often more competent to assess your organization's level of exposure to risk. The involvement of your team members in this task will depend upon both the outside resources available and their own skill sets. Their chief role will be to see that the disaster recovery plan developed actually meets the needs of your particular system. It is also up to the project team to test the plan fully, to make sure it works as expected. A complete test should be performed at least once a year.

### B.6.4    *Developing the Support Plan*

The support plan establishes a continuing, structured approach to providing technical — that is, applications — support for each user group. The support mechanism should also be able to track problems and identify trends requiring attention. If no effective support is available, you may find that the users will look for assistance with a problem, then, when they fail to find it, will try some *ad hoc* solution which only worsens the problem. Moreover, they will lose confidence in the network — a difficult mindset to overcome. In general, the best approach is to develop a practical support plan that contains a clear problem escalation process. It is also important to log all changes resulting from using the support plan in the network maintenance logs. The support plan is a particularly important strategic operational plan to monitor and keep up to date.

### B.6.5    *Developing the System Acceptance Test Plan*

The system acceptance test plan contains the criteria that will constitute acceptance of the system by the organization. It details the components of the LAN, stipulates what is to be tested, and establishes a precise methodology for testing. In brief, it outlines the hardware acceptance test plan and verifies the functional performance of the system and applications features.

The testing itself involves a site walk-through during which the LAN administrator, who is accompanied by the technology advisor or the project leader, checks all designated LAN components. The system acceptance test occurs at the end of the first activity in Phase III, site installation.

### B.6.6    *Developing the Training Plan*

Each organization develops a unique training plan. This plan is based on the training solution, which in turn is based on the training requirements assessment done during needs analysis. The training plan can be developed by the technology advisor, or by delegated in-house personnel, usually a member of the information systems group.

Whatever its details, every LAN training plan must consist of two distinct components: the training directed at the LAN administrator, and the training intended for the end users. Each of these audiences is trained at a different time. The LAN administrator's in-depth system training takes place during Phase II, prior to installation. Since the administrator functions as a member of the project team, it is important that this training be both timely and effective. The users are generally trained immediately after the LAN has been installed, during Phase III, and before the post-installation review.

### B.6.7    *Developing the Financial Plan*

The financial plan is based on information gathered during the earlier tasks in Phase I, and is therefore the final strategic operational plan developed. It details all the budgetary costs of the implementation. The financial plan is presented in two sections, entitled Financial Assumptions and Detailed Cost Breakdown. The latter section shows both capital costs and operating costs by quarter for the installation and maintenance of your LAN. It is based upon information gathered during earlier stages of Phase I. All assumptions related to the cost breakdowns are to be included in the Financial Assumptions section.

The financial plan is a vital part of the system solution report. It must be approved by management before the SSR can obtain final authorization.

## *Producing the System Solution Report (SSR)*

The system solution report is the second key deliverable of the STEPS process. Its completion is the fifth milestone in the process. The document gives detailed descriptions and specifications for the design and implementation of the proposed LAN. Having carefully read this far, you may not be able to draft this report personally, but you are aware of all the information needed to do so. You are also in a position to go back, if necessary, to any of the tasks done to date, in order to review the specifics of who performed the task, when it was completed, and how it was done.

Producing the system solution report involves the collection of all the components which have been completed to this point in the STEPS process. The following elements must be included in the report:

CHECK
LIST

✔ Functional solution summary

✔ Network overview schematic

✔ Logical network design

✔ Cabling system design

✔ Environmental and power requirements

✔ Security plan

✔ Back-up plan

✔ Disaster recovery plan

✔ Support plan

✔ System acceptance test plan

✔ Training plan

✔ Financial plan

✔ Implementation schedule

The system solution report provides the audited documentation to be used for reference throughout the implementation and after system acceptance. It simplifies making changes to the network and identifying and resolving problems. With the system solution report complete, you are ready to move on to the next activity in Phase I.

## C.   **F**UNCTIONAL DESIGN REVIEW

The third activity in Phase I is the functional design review. At this time, the system solution report is issued for a management review of its functional, technical, and financial performance. The solution is rationalized in light of management's expectations, and all discrepancies and weaknesses in it must be addressed before the project moves ahead. If problem areas are identified, an application pilot and additional cost-benefit analysis should be completed at this time and obtain management approval. This approval requires sign-off, and represents accountable agreement on the finalized solution.

It is during the functional design review that most organizations release their request for proposal. Vendor selection also takes place during this activity. The site upgrade requirements report can then be issued. This report is the third and final deliverable of Phase I of the STEPS process, and must have management approval before Phase II, installation preparation, can commence.

Figure 8.21 shows that the functional design review is comprised of three procedures: reviewing the system solution report, vendor selection, and developing the site upgrade requirements report. Each is examined in detail below.

## C.1   Reviewing the System Solution Report

Four tasks are associated with the review of the SSR: acquiring the system solution report, conducting the functional design review, changing the system solution report (if necessary), and obtaining approval for the system solution report.

### C.1.1   *Acquiring the System Solution Report*

By now you are familiar with the system solution report as an essential reference document upon which all future tasks related to the implementation must be based. It is imperative to assure both management

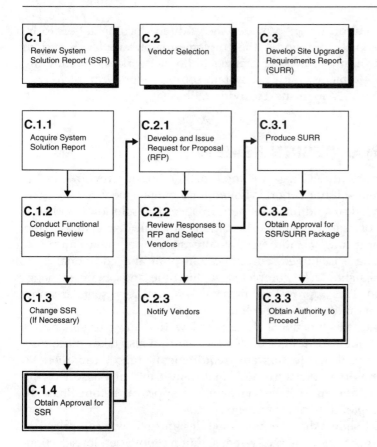

*Figure 8.21: STEPS: Process Chart For Phase I, Activity C — Functional Design Review*

and the project team that the solution will function as expected. To confirm that it will, the project team must acquire a copy of the system solution report and rationalize it in light of the proposed solution. The specifications of the solution must be examined with regard to their functional, technical, and financial performance.

### C.1.2 Conducting the Functional Design Review

In verifying the functionality of the proposed design, all discrepancies must be addressed. If any problems relating to functional or technical matters are found, then the project leader may consider developing an application pilot and a cost-benefit analysis to help resolve them. The true merit and cost-effectiveness of a proposed solution can often be identified only after one or both of these have been undertaken. Chapters 4 and 5 respectively deal with application pilots and cost-benefit analysis.

If, however, the difficulties lie in the area of finance, discussions must be held to determine whether the design should be reworked, or whether the problems can be resolved through negotiations with vendors.

### C.1.3    *Changing the System Solution Report (If Necessary)*

On the basis of either the review of the system solution report or the results of an application pilot, the project team may choose to alter some earlier recommendations. All such changes must be reflected in the final form of the SSR.

On occasion, there may be other reasons for changing a proposed solution. One possible example has to do with site management's commitment — whether formal or informal — to vendors. This situation may arise when the solution is completed only after the project has gone to tender and the organization has formally signed with a vendor. In this case, you have two design solutions to work with. Avoiding this predicament is one reason for holding off on issuing the request for proposal until the SSR has formal approval. Waiting does not guarantee that your organization will not require any additional changes to the proposed solution; however, it does serve to lessen the odds of ending up with two solutions.

If the two solutions are similar, there is little or no problem. On the other hand, if they are quite different, the project leader is responsible for resolving all difficulties before proceeding. A typical problem would be the discovery that not all applications identified in the project team's solution can be implemented in the vendor's solution. One way of coping with such a dilemma would be purchasing additional equipment. Another would be ranking your selected applications, and undertaking only a partial implementation.

However problems are resolved, all related changes must again be reflected in the final system solution report. Ongoing revisions to the SSR are necessary if it is to remain a vital and useful document.

### Obtaining Approval for the System Solution Report

The proposed solution is now ready for final approval from management. The technology advisor begins this task by reviewing the final version of the system solution report and indicating its completeness by signing off. The report is forwarded to the project leader, who also reviews it, then presents it to management. In a large implementation, a committee is usually responsible for providing authorization. When approval has been given, each authorizing manager signs the master copy of the SSR. This copy is then filed for purposes of reference and audit. A second copy is kept at the site. Management approval for the SSR is the sixth milestone in the STEPS process, and must be granted before the implementation can proceed.

## C.2    Vendor Selection

The second procedure in the functional design review is vendor selection. It involves three tasks: developing and issuing the request for proposal, reviewing responses to the RFP and selecting vendors, and notifying vendors.

### C.2.1    Developing and Issuing the Request for Proposal

The request for proposal is based on the approved solution design. It is the typical approach taken by an organization to buying products and services that exceed a price stated in the corporate policy. This document sets out your organizational, functional, and technical requirements, and solicits proposals from vendors. The more precisely you are able to specify requirements, the more appropriate the vendors' responses are likely to be. For this reason, the RFP should describe as many of your needs as possible, including all those found in the strategic operational plans.

The details of developing a request for proposal and the evaluation criteria for reviewing vendor submissions are beyond the scope of this book. If your organization has experience with this task, it has likely established a standard methodology for it. On the other hand, if your project team is uncertain as to how to develop a request for proposal, you would be well advised to seek the assistance of an experienced third party.

### C.2.2    Reviewing Responses to the RFP and Selecting Vendors

This task is particularly important, because the responses to the request for proposal are used in comparing vendors and systems. Once completed, the review results in the selection of one of more vendors.

Reviewing the responses properly requires a high level of technical and functional expertise. In a large project, the task is usually handled by a vendor selection committee made up of project team members, information systems staff, representatives of senior management, and, possibly, outside participants. In a small implementation, the project team reviews the responses and selects vendors.

Vendor selection is based upon a critical analysis of all vendors' responses according to specific evaluation criteria. These are some key points to consider when doing the comparison:

- Selection should not be made on the basis of similarities in features such as performance specifications, quality of service, and so on.

- Selection should be made on the basis of differences. The distinguishing factors are the ones which really count, which clearly show one proposal as superior to another.

- The best RFP responses will simplify your work by identifying the differences for you, either by direct comparison or by presentation.

### C.2.3   Notifying Vendors

Once the vendor of choice is named, all participating vendors should be notified. In practice, notification often follows a process of back-and-forth negotiating about any number of matters — both technical and financial — which may require adjustment before a final decision is made. The selection should then be formalized by means of a contract. Now all equipment requirements, resources, costs, and project schedules can be firmed up and appended to the system solution report.

## C.3   Developing the Site Upgrade Requirements Report (SURR)

This final procedure in the functional design review involves three tasks: producing the site upgrade requirements report, obtaining approval for the SSR/SURR package, and obtaining authority to proceed.

### C.3.1   Producing the Site Upgrade Requirements Report (SURR)

The site upgrade requirements report is the third key deliverable of the STEPS process. The document is produced by the project team once the system solution report has been finalized and approved. It lists the site upgrade requirements — that is, the changes that must be undertaken

— for the installation of the LAN proposed in the SSR. Some possible upgrades that might be required include these:

- Core drilling for cable

- Additional furnishings

- Additional electrical work

- Extra modem lines

- Mandatory UPS requirements

- Construction of walls or doors for security reasons

The project team bases the list of site upgrades on information from both the SIR and the SSR, comparing the existing site with the environment required by the proposed solution. All upgrades are indicated by highlighting the changes on each of the forms listed below. (The location of each form is indicated in brackets for your reference.)

- Network overview schematic (SSR)

- Cabling system design (SSR)

- Logical network design (SSR)

- Environmental and power requirements (SSR)

- Wiring closet information worksheets (SIR)

- Implementation schedule (SSR)

The site upgrade requirements report appears in the form of a detailed furniture and floor plan, accompanied by the relevant STEPS: Forms. It establishes a time limit within which the installation site management must hire the subcontractors needed to complete the required work. Once completed, the SURR is appended to the SSR as part of the ongoing audit and documentation process.

### C.3.2    *Obtaining Approval for the SSR / SURR Package*

After the SURR has been finalized and added to the SSR, the project leader verifies the information in the package and makes certain that it meets organizational standards. The package is then presented to management for formal approval of all upgrades, their costs, and the schedule for their completion. When the SSR/SURR package has been approved, each authorizing manager signs the master copy. This copy is filed with the project administrator; a second copy is kept at the site.

### C.3.3 Milestone    *Obtaining Authority to Proceed*

After formal approval has been granted for the SSR/SURR package, management issues a written directive to the project leader giving authorization to proceed. Completion of this task is the final milestone in Phase I, marking the end of the planning and design portion of the implementation. The project team is now ready to move on to Phase II, installation preparation.

# PHASE II:  INSTALLATION PREPARATION

## PHASE II:  INSTALLATION
## PREPARATION

The successful completion of the second phase of the STEPS process, installation preparation, is greatly dependent upon the outcome of the work done during Phase I. The main reason is that all installation preparation tasks are directly related to the approved system solution report and system upgrade requirements report, two of the key deliverables of the planning and design phase. The main objective of Phase II of the STEPS process is ensuring quality control and accountability in the physical preparation of the LAN site and equipment installation.

When Phase II is complete, your LAN site will be ready for the installation of the new system; all required equipment will have been ordered and shipped, prototyped, pre-configured, and tested. If each of these tasks is handled according to stated specifications, then the audit trail will be found in the written approval for and sign-off on the documents used in this phase: the order checklist, the prototyping report, the equipment test sign-off, and the site preparation sign-off. With these in place, the project team's only remaining preparatory tasks are training the LAN administrator and confirming the receipt of all ordered equipment at the site.

As in other parts of the STEPS process, many of the tasks described here require a certain level of technical expertise. They should be undertaken by trained personnel only. Keep in mind as you read that our chief goal in this book is to introduce you to and make you comfortable with all aspects of the implementation process.

Figure 7.1 on page 109 shows that Phase II, installation preparation, involves four activities. Chapter 9 therefore has four main sections, each corresponding to one activity: Equipment Ordering, System Prototyping, Pre-configuration and Testing, and Site Preparation. As in Chapter 8, each of these is further subdivided according to the procedures and tasks required for the completion of the activity.

## A.    **E** QUIPMENT ORDERING

You can see from Figure 9.1 that the first activity in Phase II, equipment ordering, consists of three procedures: completing purchase requisitions, placing the equipment orders, and shipping the equipment. They are discussed in turn below, in light of the tasks to be completed in each.

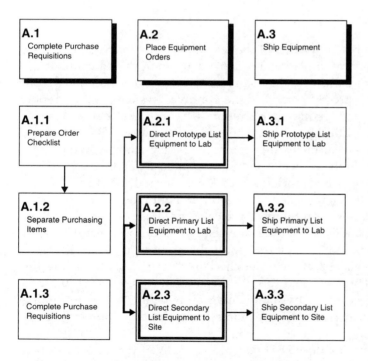

*Figure 9.1: STEPS: Process Chart for Phase II, Activity A — Equipment Ordering*

## A.1    Completing Purchase Requisitions

The first procedure associated with the ordering of equipment for your LAN implementation consists of three tasks: preparing the order checklist, separating purchasing items, and completing purchase requisitions.

### A.1.1    *Preparing the Order Checklist*

The technology advisor prepares a complete order checklist for the site installation, with the assistance of the LAN administrator. All pricing is verified with participating vendors at this time. Taking these steps "up front" helps to minimize, if not eliminate, complications in the purchasing process.

Once both the technology advisor and the LAN administrator are satisfied that the order checklist is complete and will accommodate the approved solution, each signs off on it. It is then sent to the project leader for approval before the development of purchasing forms.

It is important for this step to precede your standard organizational purchasing procedures.

### A.1.2    *Separating Purchasing Items*

Regardless of how your organization's purchasing procedures work, the STEPS process requires all equipment on the order checklist to be separated into prototype, primary, and secondary lists. Doing this is important, because the equipment on each list is shipped separately — and ideally to two different locations.

The prototype purchase list exists only if your project team determines that system prototyping is needed. It includes all items to be sent to the LAN support centre — also referred to as the lab — for system prototyping.

The primary list consists of the items to be sent to the LAN support centre for pre-configuration and testing. It includes all network equipment, such as servers, routers, gateways, and the like.

The secondary list is made up of all items not on the primary list, such as individual PCs, printers, and so on. These items are shipped directly to the LAN installation site.

The LAN support centre is the site of your future LAN support group. It may be located on or off site. It does not need to be elaborate, but should be large enough to allow the project team to set up, pre-configure, and test all new equipment.

If your organization is not in a position to allot even a small space for this lab, then the equipment on the protype and primary lists may be shipped directly to the LAN site. This is generally not a viable alternative if the installation involves a new building. In this case, you should seriously consider third-party involvement for testing, and perhaps even for ongoing support.

### A.1.3   Completing Purchase Requisitions

The responsibility for completing the standard organizational purchase requisition forms rests with either the LAN administrator or the technology advisor. It is at this point that your organization-specific purchasing procedures which precede the actual ordering should be brought into the process. If the project team has been thorough in its preliminary work, these procedures should already be included in its customized PERT charts and Gantt chart schedules.

## A.2   Placing the Equipment Orders

Of necessity, we leave the details of how to handle purchases for your organization to decide. What is important to keep in mind is that the equipment on the prototype, primary, and secondary lists must be shipped at different times, and preferably to two different places. To avoid confusion, we have broken down this procedure into three tasks to be done by your purchasing department: directing the prototype list equipment to the lab, directing the primary list equipment to the lab, and directing the secondary list equipment to the site.

 ### Directing the Prototype List Equipment to the Lab

As mentioned above, the equipment on the prototype list is purchased only if system prototyping is seen to be required. All equipment ordered for this purpose should be directed to the LAN support centre or lab, according to the schedule established for system prototyping. This is the first milestone in Phase II of the STEPS process.

 ### Directing the Primary List Equipment to the Lab

The purchasing department should direct all equipment on the primary list to the LAN support centre or lab in time for pre-configuration and testing, the third activity in Phase II. This is also a milestone in this phase of the STEPS process.

 **Directing the Secondary List Equipment to the Site**

The purchasing department should direct all equipment on the secondary list to the installation site in time to complete site preparation, the fourth and final activity in this phase. This is the third milestone in Phase II of the STEPS process.

## A.3 Shipping the Equipment

This procedure can be considered background work, because the tasks associated with it are done by the vendor rather than the project team. As might be expected, these tasks are entirely dependent upon the people involved in the ordering of equipment, and therefore occur at different times during Phase II. We include this material here to enable the project team to track all equipment orders once they have been issued. It is important for the team to be able to do this, since changes to the shipping or delivery dates will likely affect subsequent tasks.

Three tasks are involved in this procedure: shipping the prototype list equipment to the lab, shipping the primary list equipment to the lab, and shipping the secondary list equipment to the site.

### A.3.1 Shipping the Prototype List Equipment to the Lab

The vendor will have been directed to ship the prototype equipment to the LAN support centre. The shipment should be made in accordance with the date scheduled for the receipt of prototype equipment at the lab.

### A.3.2 Shipping the Primary List Equipment to the Lab

The vendor will have been directed to ship the equipment on the primary list to the lab as well. This second shipment should coincide with the date scheduled for receipt of the relevant equipment at the lab. The equipment on the primary list must arrive before pre-configuration and testing can take place.

### A.3.3    *Shipping the Secondary List Equipment to the Site*

The vendor will have been directed to ship the equipment on the secondary list to the LAN site. This final shipment should again coincide with the date established for the receipt of the relevant equipment. The equipment on the secondary list must arrive before installation, configuration, and testing can commence.

## B.    **S**YSTEM PROTOTYPING

The second activity in Phase II is system prototyping. It is done in order to check design assumptions and theories which are difficult to verify, without actually trying them out. While system prototyping is not mandatory, it is recommended in some situations.

**Prototyping** is the task of building a model in a controlled setting to see whether it works as anticipated. All new non-standard products should be examined and compared to organizational standards in this manner before being implemented. The use of a model guarantees that performance capabilities and standards are met. Special assemblies or configurations also need to be prototyped before being considered for use. For instance, prototyping is required where the design solution dictates the modification of a standard product to take account of a specific situation or application.

Figure 9.2 reveals that system prototyping consists of three procedures: configuring and assembling the prototype model, performing prototype testing, and completing the prototyping log. Each is discussed below in terms of its constituent tasks.

## B.1    Configuring and Assembling the Prototype Model

This procedure involves two tasks: developing and documenting the test methodology, and unpacking and setting up the prototype equipment.

### B.1.1    *Developing and Documenting the Test Methodology*

In preparing for system prototyping, it is essential to set objectives and test evaluation criteria at the very start. Once this has been done, a practical test procedure must be developed before prototyping is begun. Precise descriptions of all testing methods, evaluation criteria, and equipment specifications are documented in the **prototyping log**. You can see an example of this record log in Figure 9.3 (page 188).

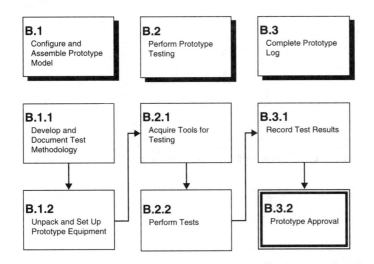

*Figure 9.2: STEPS: Process Chart for Phase II, Activity B — System Prototyping*

### B.1.2    *Unpacking and Setting Up the Prototype Equipment*

Before any test is performed, the equipment must be unpacked and set up in a designated testing area. It is important to examine the equipment and check what has been received against the packing slip.

If any of the equipment fails to function properly at this point, the vendor should be contacted immediately for an exchange. This simple action avoids confusion later on, in the event that operational difficulties arise during testing. It is handy to keep the original packaging for each piece of equipment in a safe place for later use.

Once checked, all equipment is shipped either back to the vendor or to the installation site.

## B.2    Performing Prototype Testing

The next procedure also consists of two tasks: acquiring the tools for testing, and performing the tests.

### B.2.1    *Acquiring the Tools for Testing*

Once an appropriate prototyping procedure has been settled on, it is vital to determine what software and hardware tools are required for the

# Prototyping Log

Ref ID: PTYP - 9301010002

Originator Name (Print): Jonathon Hirsh

Signature:

Date Completed: 93/08/17

## Description and Purpose

Vendor has new product called SuperWidgetABC that they say is in the final stages of becoming commercially available. It is not yet in production. We want to test it in our lab to verify that it performs to specification.

## Methodology

Assemble product in lab. Connect SuperWidgetABC to a server. Monitor the data packets being sent and the performance impacts on the server. Monitor performance on the LAN segment and on the server itself. Should this test prove that the performance decrease is not greater than .25 milliseconds, it will be considered a success.

## Results/Action Items

Performance decrease was .1 milliseconds. Successful evaluation. Recommend using it in the field.

Signing Authority: _____  Date Approved: 93/08/17

*Figure 9.3: Prototyping Log*

tests. Little more can be said about this here, since all tools used will depend entirely on the prototype being tested. If you find this gap in information disconcerting, remember that prototype testing is handled by experienced technical personnel. Assuming that your project team has been selected according to the required skill sets listed in Chapter 3, at least one member will be qualified to deal with the system prototyping issues of your implementation. It is this individual's responsibility to decide whether additional software or hardware is required for testing the prototype, as well as to obtain approval from the project leader for any necessary purchases.

### B.2.2    Performing the Tests

When all preparations are complete, testing may begin. It is imperative that the testing technicians follow all details of the test procedure, as specified in the prototyping log.

You will notice that testing occurs at various points in the STEPS process. This work is not redundant. Each testing procedure relates to specific LAN components. For example, prototype testing involves only the equipment used in creating a prototype.

## B.3    Completing the Prototyping Log

The completion of the prototyping log involves two tasks as well: recording test results, and prototype approval.

### B.3.1    Recording Test Results

For the prototype test to be effective, all results must be recorded in the prototyping log. This log serves as necessary documentation for later reference.

### B.3.2    Prototype Approval

Before the prototyping log is finalized, all the test data are forwarded to the project leader for review. If the testing was successful, the project leader will approve the prototype and sign off on the log. Prototype approval is another milestone in the STEPS process.

However, if the prototype testing was unsuccessful, the problems must be referred to the project team for further discussion and resolution.

It is essential to resolve all difficulties before the implementation proceeds. If you fail to verify standard performance issues, then regardless of the amount of documentation and accountability provided by the STEPS process, you run the risk of complications in the LAN's operation.

# C.    **P**RE-CONFIGURATION AND TESTING

The third activity in Phase II is the pre-configuration and testing of all new equipment, to ready it for installation. The installation specialist is responsible for this portion of the STEPS process. Doing pre-configuration and testing at this time, prior to Phase III, reduces the likelihood of problems during installation — as well as the potential disruption of your daily operations.

**Pre-configuration** refers to the formatting and set-up of hardware and the installation and set-up of software. Without it, your workstations and network will not function. The testing also done at this stage follows a fairly standard procedure for new equipment and applications.

You can see in Figure 9.4 that pre-configuration and testing involves five procedures: preparatory work, installing and configuring hardware, installing and configuring software, testing the equipment, and pre-configuration and testing sign-off.

## C.1    Preparatory Work

The preparatory work for pre-configuration and testing involves four tasks: unpacking equipment at the lab, sourcing reference material, reviewing the logical network design, and completing change authorization forms (if necessary).

### C.1.1    *Unpacking Equipment at the Lab*

As you read above, all equipment on the primary list is to be shipped to the LAN support centre for pre-configuration and testing. Once received, the equipment is unpacked, and, as in the case of prototype testing, the packaging is kept in a safe place for later use. Again, it is essential to examine the equipment and check what has been received against the packing slip, order forms, and purchase requisitions. Once all this has been done, the project leader initials the verified order checklist and issues a copy of it to the LAN administrator for audit purposes.

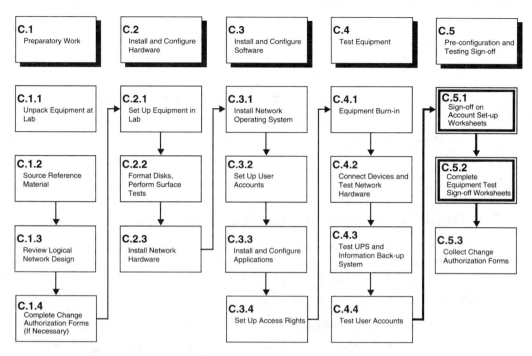

*Figure 9.4: STEPS: Process Chart for Phase II, Activity C — Pre-configuration and Testing*

### C.1.2 Sourcing Reference Material

Before undertaking the pre-configuration and testing of any equipment, it is important to source all the necessary reference documentation. This material includes the system solution report, as well as relevant technical manuals; the latter will vary with the choice of LAN design and vendor.

### C.1.3 Reviewing the Logical Network Design

Working with the system solution report, the project team reviews the logical network design before setting up for the testing of the hardware and software which follows. The logical network design gives details on how the LAN operating environment is tailored to your organization's needs. It accounts for such matters as security, directory structures, menus, log-in parameters, and so on. Reviewing the logical network design at this point should speed the configuration process. During the review, certain changes to the configuration of the network may be found necessary — for example, because of conflicts found during prototyping.

Any remaining operating system configuration worksheets, server configuration worksheets and workstation configuration worksheets are now filled in and, if need be, updated by the installation specialist.

### C.1.4   Completing Change Authorization Forms (If Necessary)

If the review of the logical network design dictates that configuration changes are, in fact, called for, then a change authorization form must be completed for each modification. The project leader must review and sign off on all change authorization forms, to authorize the changes.

## C.2   Installing and Configuring Hardware

The installation and configuration of the hardware for your LAN involves three tasks: setting up the equipment in the lab, formatting disks and performing surface tests, and installing network hardware.

### C.2.1   Setting Up the Equipment in the Lab

All the hardware is set up — as space permits — in the area designated for pre-configuration and testing.

### C.2.2   Formatting Disks and Performing Surface Tests

This task involves formatting all disks, and using special software to check for any defects on the surface of the hard disk.

### C.2.3   Installing Network Hardware

The installation specialist installs and configures the network interface cards, drivers, hubs, bridges, routers, and so forth.

## C.3   Installing and Configuring Software

The installation and configuration of the software for your LAN consists of four tasks: installing the network operating system, setting up user accounts, installing and configuring applications, and setting up access rights.

### C.3.1    Installing the Network Operating System

Before installing a network operating system such as Novell or Microsoft LAN Manager, the installation specialist must set up directory structures, as specified in the directory planning worksheets. The network operating system is then installed and configured according to the technical installation procedures detailed in the product manuals. Configuration follows the specifications established in the operating system configuration worksheets.

All workstation shell files are also created at this time. They are necessary for allowing the workstations to communicate with the network once they are installed.

### C.3.2    Setting up User Accounts

The installation specialist begins this task by setting up and customizing user accounts, log-in scripts, disk drive mapping, and applications user interfaces. The aim is to allow the end users to log in ultimately, and access various parts of the network. Some of the items established in setting up a user account include the user name and password, default login scripts, and other account-specific details. The account set-up worksheets are the source of the information used here. User accounts are set up by means of a network operating system utility.

The next step is for the installation specialist to set up the menu structures. This is done on the basis of the information contained in the menu options worksheets.

### C.3.3    Installing and Configuring Applications

The installation specialist installs and configures each piece of applications software — e.g., Microsoft Project, Microsoft Word, DELRINA PerForm PRO, Ventura Publisher, etc. — and the corresponding applications drivers. A **driver** is a piece of software which allows an application to use a particular piece of equipment, such as a printer.

Applications software is characterized as either network — licensed for shared use — or standalone — licensed for a single user. Network versions of software reside on a server, while standalone versions are found in individual workstations.

### C.3.4    Setting Up Access Rights

After the applications software has been loaded and configured, the installation specialist must establish security measures and access rights for each user. A network operating system utility is used for this task. The installation specialist assigns access rights on the basis of the information in the account set-up worksheets and security profile worksheets.

# C.4    Testing the Equipment

The equipment testing procedure is comprised of four tasks: equipment burn-in, connecting the devices and testing network hardware, testing the uninterruptable power supply (UPS) and the information back-up system, and testing user accounts.

### C.4.1    Equipment Burn-in

After all the equipment is configured, it should undergo **burn-in** for at least 24 hours — that is, it should run continuously for this period. The purpose of burn-in is to ensure that the equipment operates properly, prior to final testing. Any equipment that fails during burn-in is either repaired or replaced. It may be necessary to repeat the pre-configuration process in the event of equipment failure.

### C.4.2    Connecting the Devices and Testing Network Hardware

Once it has been determined that all the equipment works properly, the next task is connecting the server to the network. Network hardware such as network interface cards, hubs, and concentrators can then be tested. Most network operating systems provide a facility for such diagnostic testing.

### C.4.3    Testing the UPS and the Information Back-up System

The uninterruptable power supply is a vital addition to the server. This battery back-up system allows the network to continue operating in the event of a power failure. Failure to verify that the UPS is in place and operational opens your organization to the loss of important data.

Before it is tested, the UPS must be fully charged. To charge the UPS, the installation specialist connects it to the server, then to a nearby electrical outlet. Once the UPS has been fully charged, the power source is disconnected. The system is tested by being run for the specified battery life cycle.

The information back-up system was discussed in the context of the back-up plan in Chapter 6. It commonly consists of a tape back-up drive, magnetic tape, and back-up utility software. Some advanced systems use digital audio tape (DAT) or auxiliary disk back-up devices instead of magnetic tape.

Testing an information back-up system involves performing a normal back-up and restore procedure, as outlined in the approved back-up plan. Once the functionality of the system has been verified, routine maintenance checks should be made to ensure that the back-up medium is clean and not worn, and that it works properly.

### C.4.4    Testing User Accounts

It is essential to confirm that each user is properly set up in the network. Confirmation is obtained by logging in to each user account, and testing its security. If a user has the proper access rights, there should be no problem in executing any assigned application. On the other hand, if there are access restrictions on specific software, the user should not be able to access them.

## C.5    Pre-configuration and Testing Sign-off

Three tasks are involved in this procedure: signing off on the account set-up worksheets, completing the equipment test sign-off worksheets, and collecting the change authorization forms.

 ### *Signing off on the Account Set-up Worksheets*

Having completed all pre-configuration tasks and testing, the installation specialist brings the technology advisor in to review and sign the account set-up worksheets. Signing off on the account set-up worksheets is a milestone in the STEPS process. The technology advisor's sign-off confirms that each user will be able to use the system as planned.

 ### *Completing the Equipment Test Sign-off Worksheets*

The installation specialist next completes every **equipment test sign-off worksheet** (Figure 9.5), which must then be signed by the technology advisor. Sign-off on the equipment test sign-off worksheets is another

# Equipment Test Sign-off Worksheet

☑ 24 Hr. Burn-in     Notes:_____

☑ Drives Formatted/Tested   _____

☐ Hubs Tested   _____

☑ Printers Tested

☑ Back-up System Tested   _____

☐ Other:_____   _____

Ref ID: EQT - 9301010001_____

Originator Name (Print): David Sawh_____

Signature:_____

Date Completed:93/08/17_____

Device Type: Server_____

Serial #: SN000000002_____

☑ Diagnostics Completed

## Software

| Software Name | Description | Installed/Tested | Drivers Installed | Passed |
|---|---|---|---|---|
| AcctPayXX.YYY | Accounts Payable Master | ✓ | ✓ | ✓ |
| WPXXX.YYY | Word Processing Program | ✓ | ✓ | ✓ |
|  |  |  |  |  |
|  |  |  |  |  |
|  |  |  |  |  |
|  |  |  |  |  |
|  |  |  |  |  |
|  |  |  |  |  |
|  |  |  |  |  |
|  |  |  |  |  |
|  |  |  |  |  |
|  |  |  |  |  |
|  |  |  |  |  |
|  |  |  |  |  |
|  |  |  |  |  |
|  |  |  |  |  |
|  |  |  |  |  |
|  |  |  |  |  |
|  |  |  |  |  |

*Figure 9.5: Equipment Test Sign-off Worksheet*

milestone in the STEPS process. It represents certification of the quality of the equipment and software.

All pre-configured hardware and software, together with the relevant documentation, can now be shipped to the installation site.

### C.5.3    Collecting Change Authorization Forms

During pre-configuration, some alterations may be made to the system design. The technology advisor is responsible for making certain that all changes are documented and approved, that worksheets are updated, and that the system solution report reflects all changes. For audit purposes, copies of the change authorization forms and updated worksheets are appended to the SSR and forwarded to the project administrator for filing.

## D.    SITE PREPARATION

The fourth and final activity in Phase II, site preparation, is performed before the system is installed. At this time, the installation site is upgraded in accordance with the site upgrade requirements report. All the varied tasks related to the upgrade and final preparation of the physical site, as well as the training of the LAN administrator, must be completed at least one week before the system is installed. The final task is to send site management a memo confirming the readiness of the site. The LAN site is now ready for system installation.

Figure 9.6 shows that site preparation involves five procedures: installing and modifying site cabling, cable testing, making miscellaneous changes, performing electrical upgrades, and site preparation sign-off. Each procedure is examined in the sections which follow.

## D.1    Installing and Modifying Site Cabling

This procedure consists of three tasks: confirming the installation date, construction work, and installing and upgrading the cabling.

### D.1.1    Confirming the Installation Date

The date for cable installation is to be decided according to the schedule in the approved system solution report. Regardless of how the

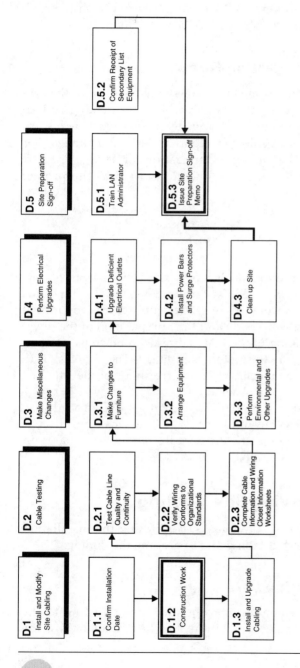

*Figure 9.6: STEPS: Process Chart for Phase II, Activity D — Site Preparation*

funding for the installation is handled, it is LAN site management, not the project team, that arranges for any cabling upgrade work. This job is typically contracted out to a firm specializing in cable installation. However, the project team retains accountability for verifying that all upgrades are properly completed before the LAN is installed.

Having the project team contact LAN site management to confirm the installation date provides an opportunity for checking that all required upgrades have been arranged. Confirming the date also saves time later on, and offers site management a face-saving way of asking for assistance, if necessary. The project leader is responsible for resolving any conflicts in scheduling.

Once the date has been confirmed, the LAN administrator notifies site staff of possible disruptions arising from cabling work. All users have to make their workstations available for upgrading and testing during the installation period.

 ## *Construction Work*

This task involves the core drilling for cable, as well as the installation of conduit, new walls, doors, and so on. It must be finished before cabling or electrical upgrades are done. The completion of construction work is a milestone in the STEPS process.

### *D.1.3   Installing and Upgrading Cabling*

You are already aware that cable is used for connecting each workstation on a LAN, as well as all communication devices such as bridges, routers, and hubs. In many installation sites, cabling is either nonexistent or inappropriate for carrying high-speed LAN traffic. As mentioned above, the task of installing building cabling usually falls to a firm that specializes in this area. Most computer or systems integration firms follow this route.

Before cabling is installed, the technology advisor must go over the cabling requirements detailed in the SURR with the contractor. The technology advisor must also be present during the installation to verify that the following details are done properly:

CHECK
LIST

✔ Connectors are placed at all cable terminations.

✔ Wall plates are used where required, and wherever possible.

✔ At least 2.5 metres of patch cable are provided for each workstation.

✔ All server zone cable runs are completed.

✔ Cable runs are properly ended at hubs and concentrator locations.

The supervisor from the cabling firm must check all work as well, and fill in both the cable information and wiring closet information worksheets — regardless of the cablers' own paperwork requirements.

## D.2    Cable Testing

Cable testing consists of three tasks: testing cable line quality and continuity, verifying that wiring conforms to organizational standards, and completing the cable information and wiring closet information worksheets.

### D.2.1    Testing Cable Line Quality and Continuity

Either the outside cable installer or your installation specialist must run continuity tests on all cable runs installed, to verify that they are functioning properly. A defective cable run will not carry signals from one workstation to another. The installer is required to replace any faulty cabling at no cost.

Existing site cabling will already have been identified on the cable information worksheets during the initial physical site inspection. Nevertheless, all cable terminations, including any existing at the site, must be accounted for on these worksheets in order to confirm that each connection has been checked.

### D.2.2    Verifying that Wiring Conforms to Organizational Standards

Once the installation and testing of cabling are complete, the technology advisor must perform a physical site inspection of the cable installer's work. The following items are to be checked:

CHECK
LIST

✔ All the necessary cables have been strung and labelled.

✔ The runs are clean, with no frayed ends or exposed or dangling cables.

✔ All cabling is terminated correctly, for example, with RJ11 twisted pair or BNC type connectors.

✔ All coaxial connectors are in place.

✔ The proper types of wiring have been used.

### D.2.3 Completing the Cable Information and Wiring Closet Information Worksheets

As noted above, the technology advisor must see that the supervisor from the cable installation firm completes and, if necessary, updates the cable information and wiring closet information worksheets. The technology advisor then has the supervisor sign off on the worksheets. This written accountability is essential for providing an audit trail of the work undertaken in this task. It is especially important at large LAN sites, where a number of installers or installation specialists may be doing the cabling. The documentation also provides valuable information in the event of subsequent upgrades to the system.

## D.3 Making Miscellaneous Changes

Miscellaneous changes to the LAN site involve the following three tasks: making changes to the furniture, arranging the equipment, and performing environmental and other upgrades.

### D.3.1 Making Changes to the Furniture

Any changes to the furniture — including location — which are called for in the site upgrade requirements report are to be completed before the installation date. The technology advisor should contact the LAN administrator no later than one week prior to that date, to confirm that such changes will be completed before the installation team arrives.

### D.3.2 Arranging the Equipment

At this time, all existing workstations and printers are placed in the proper locations, as indicated on the network overview schematic. Another important task is to place a conspicuous label stating the circuit number on each computing device equipped with a modem or telephone line. All the necessary information may be found in the SSR. Once electrical upgrades have been completed, the equipment is ready to be connected.

### D.3.3   *Performing Environmental and Other Upgrades*

It is usually the case that some last-minute environmental changes to the site — air conditioning, for instance — are required before installation can commence. Now is the time for completing them and updating all relevant documentation. Other upgrades are usually related to changes in the organization occurring between the approval of the SURR and installation preparation, such as the addition or loss of staff.

## D.4   Performing Electrical Upgrades

Three tasks must be performed here: upgrading deficient electrical outlets, installing power bars and surge protectors, and cleaning up the site.

### D.4.1   *Upgrading Deficient Electrical Outlets*

Many older sites require electrical work upgrades to accommodate a new system. The power outlets used for computing devices must be properly terminated and grounded. All nonconforming receptacles will already have been marked for upgrading in the SURR. If such upgrades are necessary, an electrical contractor should be hired to bring the site up to acceptable standards before the system is installed. It is essential for the type and quality of wire, receptacle locations, and grounding and line characteristics and condition to conform to both the local building code and the LAN equipment specifications.

### D.4.2   *Installing Power Bars and Surge Protectors*

All requirements for power bars will also have been noted in the SURR. Nevertheless, a site walk-through to review each existing and prospective workstation is in order, to make certain that each device can be properly accommodated. At least two free outlets should be available for each workstation. If any workstation lacks sufficient outlets, it should be provided with a surge protector power bar before installation. Ideally, each workstation should have a surge protector.

The need for modem line surge protectors is often overlooked. This lack results in many system burnouts caused by lightning damage.

A final precaution is to connect modems and fax machines to telephone lines by means of a telephone line protection device. The cost of all these protective devices is a small price to pay for the integrity of your system and its data.

### D.4.3   Cleaning up the Site

All debris resulting from the cabling or electrical work or the moving of equipment must be cleaned up before the site can be considered ready for LAN installation.

## D.5   Site Preparation Sign-off

The fifth and final procedure in site preparation is the sign-off. It is comprised of three tasks: training the LAN administrator, confirming the receipt of secondary list equipment, and issuing the site preparation sign-off memo.

### D.5.1   Training the LAN Administrator

The number of LAN administrators varies from project to project. To make the best use of available resources, all LAN administrators should be trained simultaneously. Their training normally takes place before or at the same time as site preparation. This training, coupled with their practical site experience, enables LAN administrators to offer considerable support during installation. Their involvement in the installation enables them to apply and practise their recently acquired knowledge, with skilled professionals at hand should assistance be necessary.

### D.5.2   Confirming the Receipt of Secondary List Equipment

The LAN administrator is responsible for confirming that all equipment on the secondary list has been received at the installation site. To ensure that it is in good order, the LAN administrator has all the equipment unpacked and checked against the packing slips. The devices must then be stored in a safe place until installation.

### D.5.3 [Milestone]   Issuing the Site Preparation Sign-off Memo

Once the LAN administrator and the technology advisor are satisfied that all tasks associated with site preparation have been properly completed, they issue the site preparation sign-off memo. This signed document is sent to the project leader and to user group management. It indicates that site preparation has been properly concluded on a specific date. This is the final milestone in Phase II of the STEPS process. A copy of the memo is attached to the SURR, for audit purposes. Now the project team is ready to commence the installation of the LAN.

CHAPTER

# 10

PHASE III: INSTALLATION

● ● ● ● ● ● ● ● ● ● ● ● ● ● ● ●

## PHASE III:  INSTALLATION

In this chapter, you will find a procedural guide to Phase III of the STEPS process, the LAN installation itself. It is designed to walk you through the installation step by step, always with a view toward project organization and accountability. Specific tasks are discussed to give you an awareness, not of their detail, but rather of how they are related to each other, and who is responsible for ensuring their success. Once again, this chapter is not intended to be a technical installation manual. Such a guide would be virtually impossible to offer here, since each organization will select equipment and a vendor most suited to its own requirements. For particulars on the installation, you should refer to the product information manuals that accompany your chosen equipment.

Despite this non-specialist orientation, parts of the chapter may still seem both technical and repetitive. The technical aspect is needed to help you become comfortable with the complexities of the installation process. The repetition is also necessary, since some of the work undertaken in Phase III will mirror the tasks associated with the pre-configuration and testing just completed. The reason for repeating certain tasks is that all equipment on your network must be configured and tested, not just the new components.

Like the tasks in Phase II, the work involved in LAN installation is the province of highly trained and experienced technical people. They may be members of your in-house staff, or, as is often the case, vendor representatives. The primary purpose of this chapter is to provide you with an effective audit process for the installation, regardless of who does the work.

If Phases I and II of the implementation have been properly done, then the installation is likely to be straightforward. Once installed, your new system can be tested. At the end of testing you will possess a complete set of documentation, for use in the event that you need to audit the process or refer to any details of the system's implementation.

Figure 7.1 on page 109 shows that Phase III, installation, involves two activities. Chapter 10 therefore has two major sections, each corresponding to one of these activities: Site Installation, and Documentation Set-up. As previously, each section is further subdivided according to the procedures and tasks required for completing the activity.

# A.    **S ITE INSTALLATION**

The first activity in Phase III, site installation, is by far the longer and more complex of the two activities which make up this phase. Figure 10.1 shows that site installation is comprised of six procedures: preparatory work, installing and configuring hardware, installing network shell files, installing and configuring applications, performing initial system testing, and system acceptance testing. They are discussed in turn below, with reference to the tasks involved in each procedure.

## A.1    **Preparatory Work**

The preparatory work for the installation of your LAN consists of four tasks: unpacking the equipment at the site, sourcing reference material, reviewing the logical network design, and reviewing the network overview schematic. Each is discussed in turn below.

### A.1.1    *Unpacking the Equipment at the Site*

You read in Chapter 9 about the pre-configuration and testing of all primary equipment at the LAN support centre or lab. Once the tasks associated with this Phase II activity are accomplished, the primary equipment is shipped to the LAN site. Also during Phase II, all secondary equipment will have been received at the site. Now, all the equipment is unpacked and set up. The technology advisor and installation

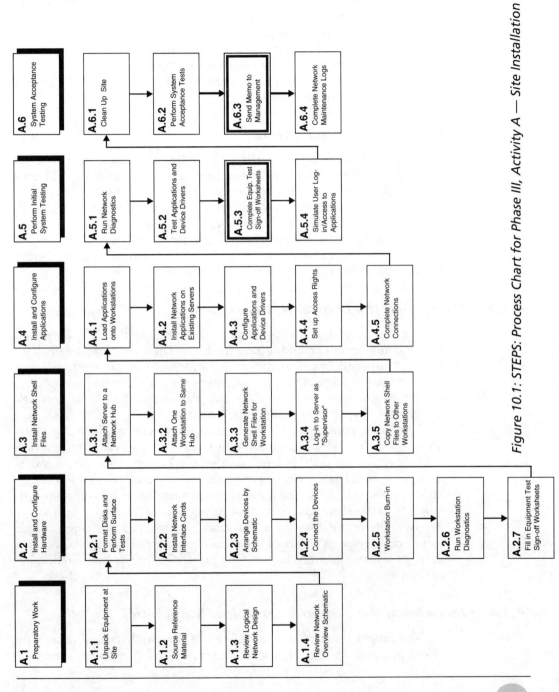

*Figure 10.1: STEPS: Process Chart for Phase III, Activity A — Site Installation*

specialist are required to undertake a physical count of the entire inventory, as well as to check that all relevant documentation is included. The prime user group co-ordinator then notifies the project leader that the primary equipment has arrived safely, and that all equipment — both primary and secondary — is accounted for. Problems such as outstanding or incorrect items should be brought to the attention of the project leader for immediate resolution.

### A.1.2   Sourcing Reference Material

Before commencing installation and testing, the project team should go over the required reference documentation. The technology advisor has the job of making sure that copies of the system solution report, the network maintenance logs, and any relevant technical manuals are available on site throughout the installation. The first of these references is the approved plan for the installation. Any significant deviation from the specifications it contains must be approved by the project leader before being implemented.

### A.1.3   Reviewing the Logical Network Design

It is also important for the project team to review the logical network design before installing and testing the LAN. This document details how the LAN operating environment is tailored to your organization's requirements, accounting for such items as security, directory structures, menus, log-in parameters, and the like. Reviewing the logical network design should speed the configuration process.

This is the point at which the installation specialist fills in any additional operating system configuration worksheets, server configuration worksheets, or workstation configuration worksheets, and updates existing ones if need be. If problems or conflicts make changes to the configuration necessary, a change authorization form must be completed to reflect both the alterations and the authorization of the project leader.

The network maintenance logs must also reflect any changes, since they form an essential part of your audit trail. From this point onward, the network maintenance logs are the major ongoing documentation for the system.

### A.1.4   Reviewing the Network Overview Schematic

The project team must also review the network overview schematic before proceeding. This high-level blueprint of the proposed layout for the work environment provides a view of the types and locations of all main LAN components and their means of interconnection. It is accompanied by a written description of the software elements in the network. The network overview schematic is especially important to the installation specialist, who is responsible for unpacking and setting up all equipment shipped to the site.

# A.2    Installing and Configuring Hardware

The second procedure in site installation is installing and configuring hardware. It involves seven tasks: formatting disks and performing surface tests, installing network interface cards, arranging the devices by schematic, connecting the devices, workstation burn-in, running workstation diagnostics, and filling in the equipment test sign-off worksheets.

## A.2.1    Formatting Disks and Performing Surface Tests

The first task associated with hardware installation and configuration involves formatting all disks for the secondary equipment. Special software is then used to check for any defects. Many vendors pre-configure and test disks before shipping them. If this is the case for your system, it is up to the project team to decide whether to perform this task.

## A.2.2    Installing Network Interface Cards

This task is the responsibility of the installation specialist. However, the technology advisor should be available throughout the installation process, in case of unforeseen difficulties.

To install NICs, the installation specialist must physically open each workstation and any existing servers at the site. Then he or she follows the configuration parameter settings outlined in the operating system configuration worksheets, server configuration worksheets, and workstation configuration worksheets.

The equipment on the primary purchase list already contains NICs. They were installed during pre-configuration and testing.

## A.2.3    Arranging the Devices by Schematic

The installation specialist verifies that all existing and new devices are located as required by the network overview schematic. The following pieces of hardware should be checked:

CHECK
LIST

✔ Servers

✔ Hubs, concentrators, bridges, routers

✔ Workstations

✔ Printers

✔ Uninterruptable power supplies

✔ Modems

The installation specialist should also make sure that the documentation for all these devices is available and up to date.

## A.2.4    Connecting the Devices

The installation specialist begins this task by plugging each UPS into the designated electrical outlet near its server. It is important to check that the UPS is properly charged; you should never assume that a UPS is charged and ready to go.

Each printer is then connected to its assigned workstation or server. Note that the PCs and any servers are not connected to the network at this point. This is done later on.

Next, the power cords from the server, workstations, printers, and hubs are plugged into the appropriate UPS or wall outlets. As each server is plugged in, the UPS signal cable is attached to the outlet on the back of the UPS card in the server. This is repeated, region by region, throughout the LAN installation site.

Communication devices, such as concentrators, bridges, routers, and the like are now connected to the network and to their designated electrical power source.

You should be aware that the network will not function until the appropriate software has been loaded, and all computing devices have been physically attached to the network.

## A.2.5    Workstation Burn-in

The workstations should be left running for at least 24 hours, to check that they operate properly before they undergo final testing. Any device that fails must be either repaired or replaced.

### A.2.6    Running Workstation Diagnostics

The installation specialist runs the diagnostic software that was shipped with the new workstations, to verify that each unit functions properly. If no diagnostic software was included, commercial utilities available for this purpose should be used. All existing and new workstations, as well as all printers, are to be tested.

### A.2.7    Filling in the Equipment Test Sign-Off Worksheets

The installation specialist is responsible for handling all configuration and testing. He or she is also required to provide documentation of this work by indicating all results on the equipment test sign-off worksheets. If any changes are found to be needed, they must be noted on the change authorization form and authorized by the project leader. They must also be recorded in the network maintenance logs.

************************

Now that the hardware-related tasks are done, the software can be installed and configured. For the sake of clarity, we have separated software configuration and installation into two procedures: installing network shell files, and installing and configuring applications.

## A.3    Installing Network Shell Files

This is the third procedure in the installation of your LAN. You may find that the description of it which follows contains some particularly specialized terminology. If you wish clarification of any of the terms, refer to the Glossary. Also keep in mind that it will be a skilled project team member or outside party who undertakes the work.

The installation of network shell files involves five tasks: attaching the server to a network hub, attaching one workstation to the hub, generating the network shell files for the workstation, logging in to the server as "Supervisor", and copying network shell files to the other workstations.

### A.3.1    Attaching the Server to a Network Hub

The installation specialist chooses one server, and attaches the LAN cable from a hub port (Port 1) to the NIC port on the back of that server.

### A.3.2    Attaching One Workstation to the Hub

The installation specialist chooses one of the workstations close to the server, and plugs in the LAN cable from the hub selected during the previous task. The server is then powered up.

### A.3.3    Generating the Network Shell Files for the Workstation

Next, the directory structure, specified in the directory planning worksheet, is set up on the chosen workstation. The default shell file is then generated by means of the network operating system's shell generation software and the corresponding workstation configurations. The latter are detailed in the workstation configuration worksheets.

Later, the default shell files will be loaded onto each workstation in the network. They allow each workstation to communicate with the network through the network interface card.

Different products typically require the use of their own shell generation/installation software. For product-specific installations, refer to the relevant utility descriptions in the appropriate product manuals.

### A.3.4    Logging in to the Server as "Supervisor"

The newly-created shell files are now copied onto a blank, formatted floppy disk — known as the shell distribution disk — for later use.

Then, using the workstation already attached to the hub, the installation specialist attempts to log in to the server as "Supervisor", or some other high-level account. (The account name to be used here varies from product to product.) Having successfully logged in, the installation specialist's next job is to change the "Supervisor" password.

### A.3.5    Copying Network Shell Files to Other Workstations

The installation specialist must now verify that all the remaining workstations are set up and capable of being connected to the network. To do this, the installation specialist uses the shell distribution disk to duplicate the LAN directory structure and workstation shells created on the original workstation on each of the other workstations.

## A.4    Installing and Configuring Applications

The fourth procedure in site installation continues the process of software installation and configuration. Installing and configuring the applications consists of five tasks: loading applications onto the workstations, installing network applications on the existing servers, configuring applications and device drivers, setting up access rights, and completing network connections.

### A.4.1 *Loading Applications onto the Workstations*

The installation specialist loads standalone applications onto each workstation, according to the specifications in the applications details worksheets and work group information worksheets.

### A.4.2 *Installing Network Applications on the Existing Servers*

Next, software identified as network applications is loaded onto the hard drives of servers already at the site. Network applications are set out in the applications details worksheets, work group information worksheets, and directory planning worksheets. It is important to keep in mind that, since all new servers will have been configured during pre-configuration in Phase II, this task applies only to the servers already in use at the site.

### A.4.3 *Configuring Applications and Device Drivers*

The installation specialist configures each piece of software (e.g., DELRINA PerForm PRO, Microsoft Word, Ventura Publisher, etc.), and its corresponding device drivers. All servers and workstations are now ready for use.

### A.4.4 *Setting Up Access Rights*

Once the applications software has been loaded and configured, the installation specialist sets up each user's access rights. A network operating system utility is used for this task. Access privileges are assigned on the basis of the account set-up worksheets and security profile worksheets.

### A.4.5 *Completing Network Connections*

The final task prior to testing the network is to confirm that all workstations and servers are physically connected and able to communicate with the network. To do this, the installation specialist walks through the site and checks that all workstations and servers are physically attached to the network by cable, wall jack, or another means. The installation specialist also confirms communication connections and proper access by logging in, then off, as a guest user at each workstation in turn.

# A.5    Performing Initial System Testing

Initial system testing involves four tasks: running network diagnostics, testing applications and device drivers, completing the equipment test sign-off worksheets, and simulating user log-in/access to the applications.

## A.5.1    *Running Network Diagnostics*

The installation specialist runs diagnostics on the network operating system, to verify that all network equipment functions properly.

## A.5.2    *Testing Applications and Device Drivers*

The technology advisor has responsibility for ensuring that all applications specified in the applications details worksheets are working properly. To verify that they are, it is necessary to log in and load every application. A test print to the appropriate printer is then performed. If there is a problem with printing, the installation specialist checks the applications drivers and prints out parameter settings to verify that they are appropriate for the destination queue. However, this eventuality should not arise, since the printers have already been tested at an earlier stage.

## A.5.3    *Completing the Equipment Test Sign-off Worksheets*

As noted above, the installation specialist is accountable for all tasks associated with installation and configuration, and for completing the equipment test sign-off worksheets. The technology advisor must then review and sign off on these documents. Signing off signifies the quality of the equipment and software.

If any changes have taken place during the installation, they will be reflected in approved change authorization forms, network maintenance logs, and the updated worksheets in the system solution report. Each of these documents will have been completed by the team member responsible, at the time the change was noted. During Phases II and III, this individual is generally the technology advisor or the installation specialist. As always, the change authorization forms require the project leader's signed approval before being forwarded to the project administrator for filing.

### A.5.4 Simulating User Log-in / Access to the Applications

The installation specialist logs in to the system, just as a user normally would. To do so, the installation specialist uses the default log-in parameters specified for each user on his or her account set-up worksheet. Once successfully logged in, the installation specialist selects and executes each menu option before exiting the selected application. Any difficulties or conflicts with the account set-up worksheet are noted in the network maintenance logs. The installation specialist should try to correct these problems at this time. All actions and results associated with problem resolution are also to be noted in the logs. The installation specialist repeats this task for each user.

## A.6 System Acceptance Testing

The final procedure in site installation is system acceptance testing. It is comprised of four tasks: cleaning up the site, performing system acceptance tests, sending a memo to management, and completing the network maintenance logs.

### A.6.1 Cleaning up the Site

Now that the installation has been completed, the project team can clean up the site. The team members should neatly package all debris, move it to a designated area, and rearrange any misplaced furniture. Finally, they should walk through the site and visually inspect the location of each device, to make sure it is properly placed and free from hazardous obstructions.

### A.6.2 Performing System Acceptance Tests

The technology advisor and the LAN administrator start this task by reviewing the system acceptance test plan and gathering the network maintenance logs and system acceptance form. They then perform a walk-through of the site. Designated network components are tested according to the system acceptance test plan, in order to demonstrate the successful operation of the installed network.

Next, the project team verifies that the LAN administrator is able to do the following:

- Manage the system

- Deal with problem escalation procedures, as outlined in the organization's LAN support plan

- Function as primary liaison with the hot-line support service

The team may have to provide the LAN administrator with some support and hand-holding until he or she is comfortable with the various tasks.

Like other acceptance procedures in the STEPS process, this one is not considered finished until all problems or conflicts are resolved. If any changes need to be made at this point, they must be included in all the appropriate documents — change authorization forms, the network maintenance logs, and updates to the SSR. When completed, all this documentation will be passed on to the project administrator.

##  *Sending a Memo to Management*

Next, the project leader meets with the LAN administrator in order to review the system acceptance plan, as set out in the SSR. Once this review is complete, the project leader sends a memo to site management. This milestone constitutes a declaration that the installation has been successfully completed. However, the memo does not constitute formal acceptance of the system. Formal system acceptance should not occur until the LAN has been fully operational for at least two months.

## A.6.4    *Completing the Network Maintenance Logs*

As stated above, any changes made by the project team during the installation must be documented in the change authorization forms and the network maintenance logs. When completed and fully approved, these documents are used to update the system solution report for audit purposes. All original signed copies are filed with the project administrator.

## B.  **D**OCUMENTATION SET-UP

The second activity in Phase III is documentation set-up. Clearly, among the most essential elements in the STEPS process are the tracking and accountability built in for each task. Before installation may be considered complete, all documentation must be set up and made available at the user site. You have just read about one element needed for accomplishing this, the inclusion of all changes in the system solution report by the end of testing. Another vital piece of documentation is the procedures manual, which describes how to use the system. These two documents, the SSR and the procedures manual, are the key deliverables in Phase III.

It is also at this time that additional support documents, notably a customized LAN user guide, will be developed for use in the end user training which takes place before the post-installation review in Phase IV.

You can see in Figure 10.2 that documentation set-up consists of just one procedure, finalizing documentation. It is discussed below, in light of the six tasks associated with it.

## B.1   **Finalizing Documentation**

This procedure involves six tasks: organizing the documentation, developing the customized LAN user guide, reviewing the documentation, filing the documentation, confirming trainer selection and training session dates, and end user training.

### B.1.1   *Organizing the Documentation*

Throughout the implementation, the project administrator has served as the repository for all original documents. At each step of the process, the project team will have ensured that the necessary authorizations have been obtained and sign-off provided. By doing this, the team has produced your trail of accountability.

It is now the task of the project administrator to gather all relevant information and generate closing documentation detailing the installation and support resources available for the site. This background material includes the following items:

- Sample back-up logs

- Completed network maintenance logs

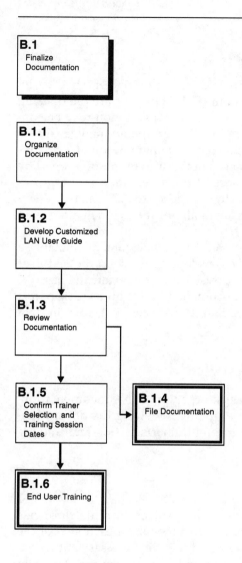

*Figure 10.2: STEPS: Process Chart for Phase III, Activity B — Documentation Set-up*

- Completed change authorization forms

- System and applications procedure manuals

- System solution report

### B.1.2    Developing the Customized LAN User Guide

Using the project administrator's finalized documentation, the technology advisor must now prepare a brief customized LAN user guide for your organization. It is intended to cover all areas about which the end users may require information, including these:

- The content of the documentation, and where this information can be found

- General administrative procedures: back-ups, security, user set-ups, error log checks, and so on

- Preventive maintenance

- Problem resolution

### B.1.3    Reviewing the Documentation

Next, the technology advisor reviews the system solution report and change authorization forms with the LAN adminstrator. This task is done primarily to ensure that the site personnel are familiar with the following:

- Functional solution summary

- The components of the LAN

- Cabling diagrams and cabling topology

- Back-up procedures and preventive maintenance

- Support plans and problem escalation procedures

- Disaster recovery plans

- The training plan and the LAN user guide

- A general overview of the available documentation

## Filing the Documentation

With the development of the user guide and the finalization of installation and worksheet updates in the SSR, the installation documentation is complete. This is another milestone in the STEPS process. The documentation is filed at both the LAN support centre and the installation site for reference purposes.

## B.1.5 Confirming Trainer Selection and Training Session Dates

For any LAN implementation to be a success, the end users must be comfortable with the system. The STEPS process makes every reasonable effort to involve the users in the implementation. This is particularly true in the planning and design phase, where their involvement gives them the opportunity to start to understand the changes which are being considered in their work environment. After this initial phase, however, the involvement of the users is typically limited by the highly technical nature of the tasks to be done.

Once installation is underway, the users begin to see the reality of what is taking place and often require reassurance. Confirming the selection of a trainer and arranging the dates for training sessions are good ways of providing this encouragement. Chapters 3 and 6 offer more detailed information on trainers' requisite skill sets and trainer selection, as well as the arrangement of training courses.

## End User Training

End user training sessions are designed according to the customized training plan found in the SSR. They are generally held on a group basis sometime after LAN installation begins. Their timing depends greatly on the available resources. For instance, training for specific applications, such as word processing, can be offered off site prior to installation. On the other hand, it is more effective to introduce LAN-related sessions only when facilities actually exist at the site.

At the most basic level of training, the trainer teaches users log-in procedures, reviews general LAN architecture and use, and demonstrates how and where to get assistance with such matters as accessing local and remote printers and servers, and using desktop applications and databases. Depending on the site, the trainer may have to demonstrate the use of more complex network elements such as gateways and modems. Again, more detail on training course material can be found in Chapter 6.

PHASE IV: POST-INSTALLATION

. . . . . . . . . . . . . . . . . . . . . . . . . .

# CHAPTER 11

# PHASE IV: POST-INSTALLATION

In Phase IV of the STEPS process, the project team ensures that the LAN implementation does, in fact, pull together. As "post-installation" implies, your new system will have been in full operation for some time, and actual operational results will have started to surface.

The tasks associated with post-installation are designed primarily to verify that your LAN is functioning as expected. To meet this goal, it is important both to hold orientation sessions and to do a post-installation review. In complex implementations, it may be hard to determine problem areas. The meetings and review enable the project team to address several important tasks before formal system acceptance, including these:

- Providing user orientation

- Ascertaining the users' level of comfort in using the new system

- Identifying and dealing with areas requiring further refinement

- Dealing with issues associated with problem resolution

- Confirming that all strategic operational plans are in place and working as intended

- Arranging to hand operational responsibility over to site management

The sessions also give users the chance to discuss the exciting opportunities opening up as a result of the LAN implementation: changing roles, new responsibilities, increased effectiveness, and so forth.

Although all these events take place after the new system has been installed, keep in mind that the preparatory work for post-installation actually begins at the outset of the project. Developing the training and support plans is an example of such preliminary work. If your LAN is to succeed — particularly in the eyes of the users — the preparation in the first three phases must be properly done.

Figure 7.1 on page 109 shows that Phase IV, post-installation, involves three activities. Chapter 11 is therefore divided into three main sections, each corresponding to one of these activities: Orientation and Initial Support, Post-Installation Review, and Formal System Acceptance. As in the three previous chapters, each section is further subdivided according to the procedures and tasks required for completing the activity.

## A. ORIENTATION AND INITIAL SUPPORT

The first activity in Phase IV is orientation and initial support. You can see in Figure 11.1 that it consists of just one procedure, holding the orientation sessions.

## A.1 Holding the Orientation Sessions

This procedure is comprised of three tasks: scheduling the orientation review sessions, user orientation, and LAN administrator orientation. Each is discussed in turn below.

### A.1.1 Scheduling the Orientation Review Sessions

It is the responsibility of the technology advisor to arrange post-installation orientation review sessions for the LAN administrator and the end users. A separate session is usually held for the LAN administrator, since operations must be covered at a more technical and detailed level for this individual. The review sessions should be scheduled in conjunction with site management, to cause least disruption to the users.

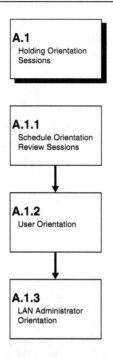

*Figure 11.1: STEPS: Process Chart for Phase IV, Activity A — Orientation and Initial Support*

### A.1.2    User Orientation

User orientation is intended to acquaint the end users with the broader issues associated with their LAN, as opposed to the specifics of their individual workstations and applications, with which they are already somewhat familiar. Using the finalized documentation and the customized user guide developed in Phase III, the technology advisor goes over the following areas:

- The content of the documentation, and where this information can be found

- General administrative procedures: back-ups, security, user set-ups, error log checks, and so on

- Preventive maintenance

- Problem resolution

Having been introduced to these matters, all participants in the session will be given a copy of the LAN user guide for reference.

### A.1.3    LAN Administrator Orientation

The LAN administrator has already gone over the matters covered during user orientation. It is now necessary for the technology advisor to tell the LAN administrator about the finer details of the system, as well as to inform him or her about the steps involved in its administration. The following topics are typically covered at this session:

CHECK
LIST

✔ Routine server maintenance

✔ The procedure for rebooting a downed server

✔ Back-up procedures

✔ Maintenance and technical support set-up and procedures

✔ E-mail and remote access gateways

✔ Procedure manuals

✔ Applications installation, modification, and troubleshooting

✔ Printer control and use

## B.    **P**OST-INSTALLATION REVIEW

The second activity in Phase IV is the post-installation review. Figure 11.2 shows that it also consists of a single procedure.

## B.1    Conducting the Post-Installation Review

Five tasks are involved in this procedure: scheduling the post-installation review, reviewing the problems logged to date, holding post-installation review sessions, performing minor repairs, and updating the documentation.

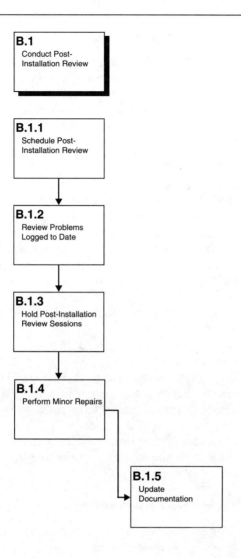

*Figure 11.2: STEPS: Process Chart for Phase IV, Activity B — Post-Installation Review*

### B.1.1    Scheduling the Post-Installation Review

Shortly after the network is installed, the technology advisor sends a memo to the LAN administrator to arrange a site visit. Its purpose is to allow these team members to check the operation of the system. The visit typically takes place during the first four to six weeks of the LAN's operation.

### B.1.2    Reviewing the Problems Logged to Date

Before the site visit, the technology advisor reviews the network maintenance logs at the LAN support centre. Since the LAN is an entirely new environment for many end users, there is likely to be a wide array of problems during the first month of operation. All of them should be noted and dealt with by the LAN administrator. As always, details of the problems and their resolution are added to the network maintenance logs, then forwarded to the lab. This should be done weekly during the first two months of operation, and monthly from then on. However, all critical problems must be logged and called in without delay, for immediate resolution.

The problems logged in the early period of the LAN's operation must be carefully examined and classified, under such headings as Workstations, Software, System Login Script, and so on. Distinguishing trends and common occurrences makes it easier to isolate difficulties and classify them as either technical "bugs" to be fixed by the vendor, or problems caused by improper use of the system. This information helps the technology advisor in identifying further training needs and possible design-related modifications. It also helps in conducting the post-installation review sessions which follow.

### B.1.3    Holding Post-Installation Review Sessions

Every successful implementation has tremendous potential for new opportunities and growth. A well-implemented LAN will quickly become an operational tool which the end users come to rely upon. However, if at any point, particularly when the system is new, the network fails to function as expected or is difficult to work with, the users typically become unforgiving and lose faith rapidly.

To prevent this undesirable situation, it is important for the technology advisor to hold at least one post-installation review session. It gives both the users and the LAN administrator a forum for airing their problems and working through them. The session also helps the project team evaluate the effectiveness of the implementation on a continuing basis.

### B.1.4    *Performing Minor Repairs*

Change requests recorded in the network maintenance logs, as well as those determined at the review sessions, are to be taken to LAN site management for approval. Once they are approved, the project team arranges for the repairs to be done.

### B.1.5    *Updating the Documentation*

As at every point in the STEPS process, any adjustments to the system must be noted and authorized before the implementation can continue. Here, it is the responsibility of the project leader to update the system solution report so that it reflects these changes.

## C.    **F**ORMAL SYSTEM ACCEPTANCE

The third activity in Phase IV, and the final activity in the STEPS process, is formal system acceptance. Your implementation can be considered complete only after this has taken place, when the LAN has been operating for a specific period.

Figure 11.3 shows that formal system acceptance is comprised of one procedure.

## C.1    System Acceptance Sign-off

This final procedure consists of four tasks: waiting out the acceptance period, reviewing the network maintenance logs, the acceptance review, and the formal system acceptance sign-off.

### C.1.1    *Waiting out the Acceptance Period*

This task consists basically of taking a "wait and see" attitude. The time that should elapse before formal acceptance varies with the complexity of the system, as well as with whom you ask. In our experience, waiting two to six months after the installation of the LAN is advisable. A period of several months allows the end users and the LAN administrator to become accustomed to the network and its operations. It also provides an opportunity for looking objectively at the problems which surface, as well as for testing the effectiveness of the support plan.

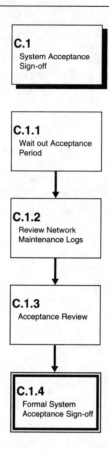

*Figure 11.3: STEPS: Process Chart for Phase IV, Activity C — Formal System Acceptance*

### C.1.2 Reviewing the Network Maintenance Logs

The network maintenance logs have already been reviewed once, during the post-installation review procedure. This second review consolidates information about trends and common problems. It is essential to resolve these issues before the acceptance review that follows, in order to evaluate the LAN realistically.

### C.1.3 Acceptance Review

The acceptance review meeting is held some time after the post-installation review. It is usually attended by LAN site management, the project leader, the technology advisor, and a vendor representative. This group has the responsibility of reviewing all the relevant material and making the final decision as to whether the LAN should receive formal system acceptance. The group convenes when all other tasks in the STEPS process have been properly completed. The documentation is in order, the strategic operational plans are in use, and the LAN has been running for at least two months.

## C.1.4 Milestone — *Formal System Acceptance Sign-off*

This sign-off is the final key deliverable in the STEPS process. Only after all of the following have taken place can you or your delegate sign off on formal LAN acceptance:

- The approved system acceptance test plan has been successfully undertaken.

- Your organization has had the opportunity to use the system, at full operation, for at least two months.

- The performance of your LAN has been reviewed, and the system has been found to be providing the anticipated results.

Now you can provide the formal system acceptance sign-off, which officially marks the successful completion of your LAN implementation.

**************************

But this is by no means the end. Throughout this book, we have repeatedly pointed out that your LAN and its customized strategic operational plans form a dynamic system. To operate at peak effectiveness, they must be constantly monitored, re-assessed, and adjusted to account for growth, refinements, and technological and functional changes.

Furthermore, the procedures outlined in this volume offer you both direction and an organized, consistent approach for more than LAN implementation. They may readily be adapted, in part or in whole, for ongoing use. By employing the STEPS: Forms and STEPS: Reports, and adjusting the process charts to meet your new needs, you should with ease be able to establish a customized STEPS system for your organization. This system is designed for project tracking, reporting, documentation, and, where necessary, implementation revisions. If you have employed the STEPS: Tools software, you will already have in place an automated documentation database from which to begin, and a methodology to help you manage your operations. In this way, you are making the fullest possible use of STEPS.

A client of ours once summed up the benefits of the STEPS process in these words: "You know, people in my organization come and go. When people leave or I bring in new staff — even in the middle of a project — I now have good documentation and a systematic process, to keep things going smoothly."

● ● ● ● ● ● ● ● ● ● ● ● ● ● ● ● ● ● ● ● ● ● ● ●

# APPENDIX

# A

# STEPS: Process Charts

# The Four Phases of the STEPS Process, and Dependent Activities

**Phase I:**
Planning and Design

**A.** Project Start-up

**B.** Technical Requirements and Design

**C.** Functional Design Review

**Phase II:**
Installation Preparation

**A.** Equipment Ordering

**B.** System Prototyping

**C.** Pre-configuration and Testing

**D.** Site Preparation

**Phase III:**
Installation

**A.** Site Installation

**B.** Documentation Set-up

**Phase IV:**
Post-Installation

**A.** Orientation and Initial Support

**B.** Post-Installation Review

**C.** Formal System Acceptance

# Process Chart for Phase I, Activity A — Project Start-up

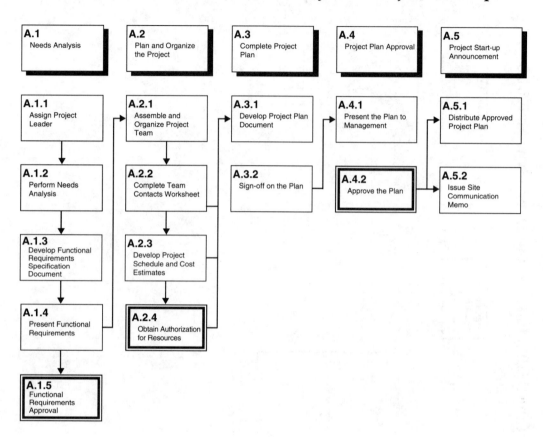

# Process Chart for Phase I, Activity B — Technical Requirements and Design

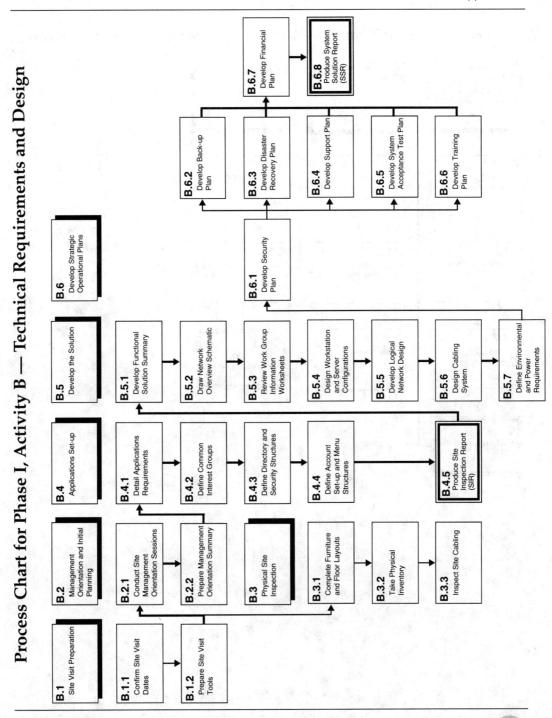

# Process Chart for Phase I, Activity C — Functional Design Review

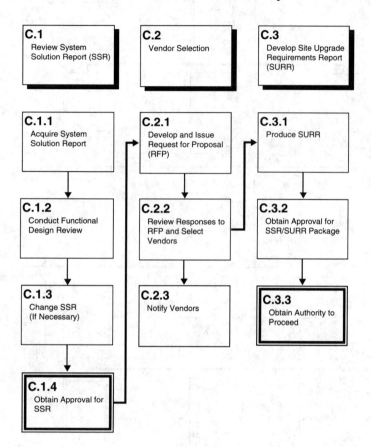

**C.1**
Review System
Solution Report (SSR)

**C.2**
Vendor Selection

**C.3**
Develop Site Upgrade
Requirements Report
(SURR)

**C.1.1**
Acquire System
Solution Report

**C.2.1**
Develop and Issue
Request for Proposal
(RFP)

**C.3.1**
Produce SURR

**C.1.2**
Conduct Functional
Design Review

**C.2.2**
Review Responses to
RFP and Select
Vendors

**C.3.2**
Obtain Approval for
SSR/SURR Package

**C.1.3**
Change SSR
(If Necessary)

**C.2.3**
Notify Vendors

**C.3.3**
Obtain Authority to
Proceed

**C.1.4**
Obtain Approval for
SSR

# Process Chart for Phase II, Activity A — Equipment Ordering

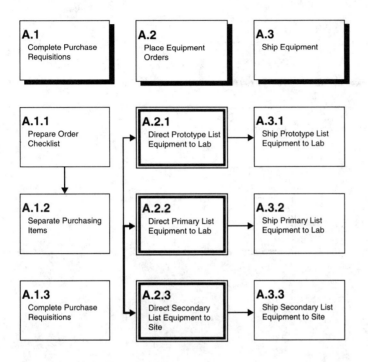

## Process Chart for Phase II, Activity B — System Prototyping

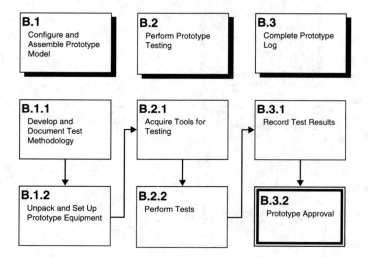

**B.1**
Configure and
Assemble Prototype
Model

**B.2**
Perform Prototype
Testing

**B.3**
Complete Prototype
Log

**B.1.1**
Develop and
Document Test
Methodology

**B.2.1**
Acquire Tools for
Testing

**B.3.1**
Record Test Results

**B.1.2**
Unpack and Set Up
Prototype Equipment

**B.2.2**
Perform Tests

**B.3.2**
Prototype Approval

# Process Chart for Phase II, Activity C — Pre-configuration and Testing

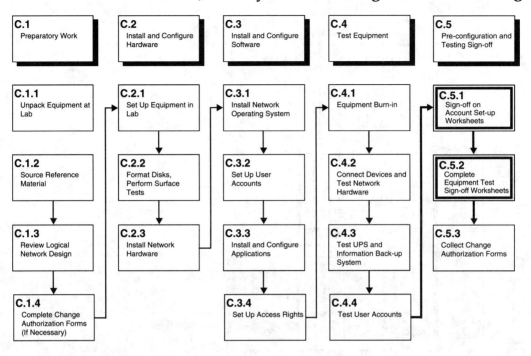

# Process Chart for Phase II, Activity D — Site Preparation

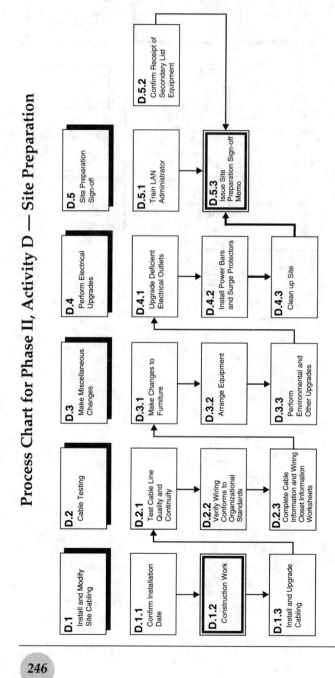

# Process Chart for Phase III, Activity A — Site Installation

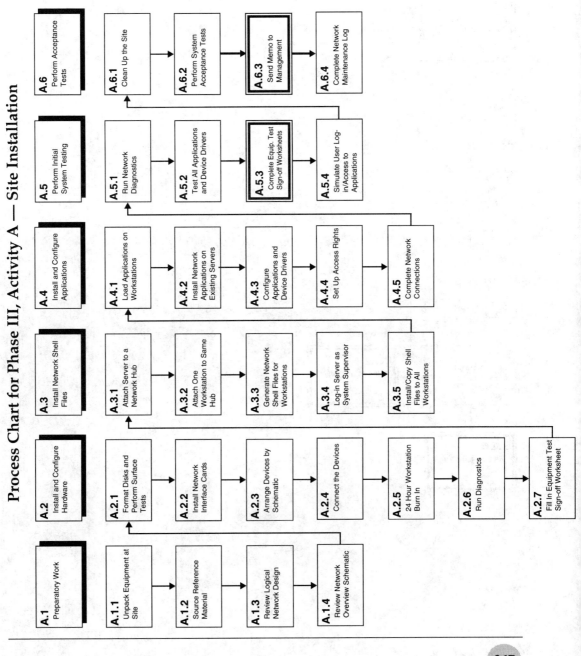

**A.1** Preparatory Work

- **A.1.1** Unpack Equipment at Site
- **A.1.2** Source Reference Material
- **A.1.3** Review Logical Network Design
- **A.1.4** Review Network Overview Schematic

**A.2** Install and Configure Hardware

- **A.2.1** Format Disks and Perform Surface Tests
- **A.2.2** Install Network Interface Cards
- **A.2.3** Arrange Devices by Schematic
- **A.2.4** Connect the Devices
- **A.2.5** 24 Hour Workstation Burn In
- **A.2.6** Run Diagnostics
- **A.2.7** Fill In Equipment Test Sign-off Worksheet

**A.3** Install Network Shell Files

- **A.3.1** Attach Server to a Network Hub
- **A.3.2** Attach One Workstation to Same Hub
- **A.3.3** Generate Network Shell Files for Workstations
- **A.3.4** Log-in Server as System Supervisor
- **A.3.5** Install/Copy Shell Files to All Workstations

**A.4** Install and Configure Applications

- **A.4.1** Load Applications on Workstations
- **A.4.2** Install Network Applications on Existing Servers
- **A.4.3** Configure Applications and Device Drivers
- **A.4.4** Set Up Access Rights
- **A.4.5** Complete Network Connections

**A.5** Perform Initial System Testing

- **A.5.1** Run Network Diagnostics
- **A.5.2** Test All Applications and Device Drivers
- **A.5.3** Complete Equip. Test Sign-off Worksheets
- **A.5.4** Simulate User Log-in/Access to Applications

**A.6** Perform Acceptance Tests

- **A.6.1** Clean Up the Site
- **A.6.2** Perform System Acceptance Tests
- **A.6.3** Send Memo to Management
- **A.6.4** Complete Network Maintenance Log

# Process Chart for Phase III, Activity B — Documentation Set-up

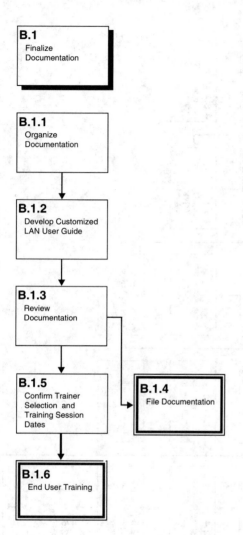

# Process Chart for Phase IV, Activity A — Orientation and Initial Support

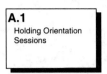

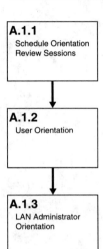

# Process Chart for Phase IV, Activity B — Post-Installation Review

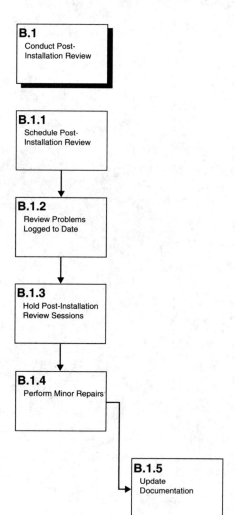

**B.1**
Conduct Post-Installation Review

**B.1.1**
Schedule Post-Installation Review

**B.1.2**
Review Problems Logged to Date

**B.1.3**
Hold Post-Installation Review Sessions

**B.1.4**
Perform Minor Repairs

**B.1.5**
Update Documentation

# Process Chart for Phase IV, Activity C — Formal System Acceptance

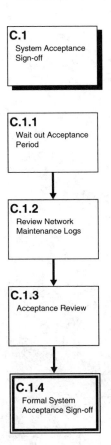

# APPENDIX

# B

## STEPS: Forms

# APPENDIX B

Appendix B contains two components: a STEPS: Forms Cross Reference List, and sample copies of all the forms illustrated and discussed in the body of *STEPS for Implementing Local Area Networks*. To make it easier for you to locate any given form, the STEPS: Forms Cross Reference List is presented first.

This cross-reference consists of four tables, which correspond to the four phases of the STEPS process. Within each table, all forms mentioned in the book are listed in alphabetical order down the left-hand side. The activities which make up each phase of the process appear across the top of the appropriate table. Each form is then referenced under the activity or activities during which it is used.

As an example, suppose that you need to find out quickly which form or forms to use during the first activity of the STEPS process, project start-up. Turn to the first table in the STEPS: Forms Cross Reference List, on the next page. Look at the top of the table, where the heading Project Start-up appears. By scanning down the page under this heading, you can see that the activity involves four forms: the change authorization form, end user profile worksheet, project status report, and team contacts worksheet.

The sample copies of all the forms referred to within the body of this book appear in alphabetical order after the STEPS: Forms Cross Reference List.

# STEPS: Forms Cross Reference List

## Phase I: Planning and Design

| Worksheets and Forms | Project Start-up | Technical Requirements and Design | Functional Design Review |
|---|:---:|:---:|:---:|
| Account Set-up Worksheet | | ● | ● |
| Applications Details Worksheet - Commercial | | ● | ● |
| Applications Details Worksheet - Custom | | ● | ● |
| Back-up Log | | ● | ● |
| Cable Information Worksheet | | ● | ● |
| Change Authorization Form | ● | ● | ● |
| Directory Planning Worksheet | | ● | ● |
| End User Profile Worksheet | ● | ● | ● |
| Equipment Summary Worksheet | | ● | ● |
| Equipment Test Sign-off Worksheet | | | |
| Menu Options Worksheet | | ● | ● |
| Network Applications Summary Worksheet | | ● | ● |
| Network Maintenance Log | | ● | ● |
| Operating System Configuration Worksheet | | ● | ● |
| Project Status Report | ● | ● | ● |
| Prototyping Log | | | |
| Security Profile Worksheet | | ● | ● |
| Server Configuration Worksheet | | ● | ● |
| Team Contacts Worksheet | ● | ● | ● |
| Wiring Closet Information Worksheet | | ● | ● |
| Work Group Information Worksheet | | ● | ● |
| Workstation Configuration Worksheet | | ● | ● |

# STEPS: Forms Cross Reference List

## Phase II:  Installation Preparation

| Worksheets and Forms | Equipment Ordering | System Prototyping | Pre-configuration and Testing | Site Preparation |
|---|---|---|---|---|
| Account Set-up Worksheet | ● | Depending on the prototype tested, some or most of these forms are used. | ● | |
| Applications Details Worksheet - Commercial | ● | | | |
| Applications Details Worksheet - Custom | ● | | ● | |
| Back-up Log | | Not used | ● | |
| Cable Information Worksheet | ● | Possibly | ● | ● |
| Change Authorization Form | ● | Always useful when testing | ● | ● |
| Directory Planning Worksheet | ● | Possibly | ● | |
| End User Profile Worksheet | ● | Possibly | ● | |
| Equipment Summary Worksheet | ● | Possibly | ● | ● |
| Equipment Test Sign-off Worksheet | | A necessity for prototype tests | | |
| Menu Options Worksheet | ● | Possibly | ● | |
| Network Applications Summary Worksheet | ● | Possibly | ● | |
| Network Maintenance Log | | Not used | ● | |
| Operating System Configuration Worksheet | | Possibly | ● | |
| Project Status Report | ● | Ongoing documentation | ● | ● |
| Prototyping Log | | A necessity for prototype tests | | |
| Security Profile Worksheet | | Possibly | ● | |
| Server Configuration Worksheet | ● | Possibly | ● | |
| Team Contacts Worksheet | ● | Used throughout | ● | ● |
| Wiring Closet Information Worksheet | ● | Possibly | ● | ● |
| Work Group Information Worksheet | ● | Possibly | ● | |
| Workstation Configuration Worksheet | ● | Possibly | ● | |

# STEPS: Forms Cross Reference List

## Phase III:  Installation

| Worksheets and Forms | Site Installation | Documentation Set-up |
|---|:---:|:---:|
| Account Set-up Worksheet | • | • |
| Applications Details Worksheet - Commercial | • | • |
| Applications Details Worksheet - Custom | • | • |
| Back-up Log | • | • |
| Cable Information Worksheet | • | • |
| Change Authorization Form | • | • |
| Directory Planning Worksheet | • | • |
| End User Profile Worksheet | • | • |
| Equipment Summary Worksheet | • | • |
| Equipment Test Sign-off Worksheet | • | • |
| Menu Options Worksheet | • | • |
| Network Applications Summary Worksheet | • | • |
| Network Maintenance Log | • | • |
| Operating System Configuration Worksheet | • | • |
| Project Status Report | • | • |
| Prototyping Log | | • |
| Security Profile Worksheet | • | • |
| Server Configuration Worksheet | • | • |
| Team Contacts Worksheet | • | • |
| Wiring Closet Information Worksheet | • | • |
| Work Group Information Worksheet | • | • |
| Workstation Configuration Worksheet | • | • |

# STEPS: Forms Cross Reference List

## Phase IV:  Post-Installation

| Worksheets and Forms | Orientation and Initial Support | Post-Installation Review | Formal System Acceptance |
|---|:---:|:---:|:---:|
| Account Set-up Worksheet | | | |
| Applications Details Worksheet - Commercial | ● | | |
| Applications Details Worksheet - Custom | ● | | |
| Back-up Log | ● | ● | ● |
| Cable Information Worksheet | | | |
| Change Authorization Form | ● | ● | ● |
| Directory Planning Worksheet | | | |
| End User Profile Worksheet | ● | | |
| Equipment Summary Worksheet | | | |
| Equipment Test Sign-off Worksheet | | | |
| Menu Options Worksheet | | | |
| Network Applications Summary Worksheet | ● | | |
| Network Maintenance Log | ● | ● | ● |
| Operating System Configuration Worksheet | | | |
| Project Status Report | ● | ● | ● |
| Prototyping Log | | | |
| Security Profile Worksheet | | | |
| Server Configuration Worksheet | | | |
| Team Contacts Worksheet | ● | ● | ● |
| Wiring Closet Information Worksheet | | | |
| Work Group Information Worksheet | | | |
| Workstation Configuration Worksheet | | | |

# Account Set-up Worksheet

User Name/ID: Robert Quadrini /RQTOWNE

Group Name/ID: Accounts Payable/AP

Organization Name/ID: Finance/FIN

Electronic Mail ID: FIN/AP/RQTOWNE

Ref ID: ASW - 9301010001

Originator Name (Print): Choi Wai Luon

Signature:

Date Completed:93/08/14

## Default Settings

Date Account Expires(YY/MM/DD): **93/12/05**
Max. Connections: 2
Min. Password Length: 5
# Log-ins Allowed: 3
Max Disk Space (Mb): 150

Require Unique            ☑ Yes        ☐ No

| | | | | |
|---|---|---|---|---|
| Restrict Sign-on Between _12:00 am_ | to | _12:00 pm_ | on | Sat, Sun |
| Restrict Sign-on Between _6:30 pm_ | to | _8:00 am_ | on | Mon-Fri |
| Restrict Sign-on Between _____ | to | _____ | on | _____ |
| Restrict Sign-on Between _____ | to | _____ | on | _____ |
| Restrict Sign-on Between _____ | to | _____ | on | _____ |
| Restrict Sign-on Between _____ | to | _____ | on | _____ |

(Time=HH:MMam)

## Application Access

| Application Name/Path | Read Only | Read/ Write | Write Only | Note |
|---|---|---|---|---|
| G:\FIN\ACCPAY\AcctPayXX.YYY | | ✓ | | Payables Clerk |
| F:\CORP\EMAIL | | ✓ | | Corporate Electronic Mail |
| | | | | |
| | | | | |
| | | | | |
| | | | | |
| | | | | |
| | | | | |
| | | | | |
| | | | | |
| | | | | |
| | | | | |

# Applications Details Worksheet
## - Commercial -

Ref ID: APP - 9301010001

Originator Name (Print): Choi Wai Luon

Signature:

Date Completed:93/08/07

*Commercial Applications*

| Application Name | Version | LAN Version | # of Nodes | Size (Mb) | Main Use |
|---|---|---|---|---|---|
| WordProcess | 5.1 | ✓ | 25 | 2 | Word Processing - correspondence |
| | | | | | |
| | | | | | |
| | | | | | |
| | | | | | |
| | | | | | |
| | | | | | |
| | | | | | |
| | | | | | |
| | | | | | |
| | | | | | |
| | | | | | |
| | | | | | |

*Special Set-up Instructions*

| Application Name | Instructions |
|---|---|
| | |
| | |
| | |
| | |
| | |
| | |

# Applications Details Worksheet
## - Custom -

Ref ID: APP - <u>9301010001</u>

Originator Name (Print): <u>Choi Wai Luon</u>

Signature:_____

*Custom Applications*

Date Completed:<u>93/08/07</u>

| Application Name | Version | LAN Version | # of Nodes | Size (Mb) | Main Use |
|---|---|---|---|---|---|
| AcctPayXX.YYY | 1.0 | ✓ | 25 | 2 | Data Entry For Payables |
| Inventry.YYY | 3 | ✓ | 5 | 1 | Inventory Master |
|  |  |  |  |  |  |
|  |  |  |  |  |  |
|  |  |  |  |  |  |
|  |  |  |  |  |  |
|  |  |  |  |  |  |
|  |  |  |  |  |  |
|  |  |  |  |  |  |
|  |  |  |  |  |  |
|  |  |  |  |  |  |
|  |  |  |  |  |  |
|  |  |  |  |  |  |
|  |  |  |  |  |  |

*Special Set-up Instructions*

| Application Name | Instructions |
|---|---|
| AcctPayXX.YYY | Make Sure Buffers are set to at least 32 in Config.Sys |
|  |  |
|  |  |
|  |  |
|  |  |
|  |  |

# Back-up Log

Ref ID: BL - <u>930101000</u>

Server ID:  <u>ServerX</u>

Location:  <u>2B1</u>

Server Function:  <u>Accounting Files</u>

*Audit Trail*

| Tape ID | Date/Time | Back-up Type (Full/Incremental) | Backed Up By | Notes |
|---------|-----------|--------------------------------|--------------|-------|
| 93D0001 | 93/01/21 | Full | M. Miller | Daily Back-up |
| 93D0002 | 93/01/22 | Full | M. Miller | Daily Back-up |
| 93D0003 | 93/01/25 | Full | M. Miller | Daily Back-up |
| 93D0004 | 93/01/26 | Full | M. Rubin | Daily Back-up |
| 93D0005 | 93/01/27 | Full | M. Rubin | Daily Back-up |
| 93D0006 | 93/01/28 | Full | M. Rubin | Daily Back-up |
| 93D0007 | 93/01/29 | Full | M. Rubin | Daily Back-up |
| 93M0001 | 93/01/31 | Full | J. Franco | Monthly Back-up |
| 93D0001 | 93/02/01 | Full | J.Franco | Daily Back-up |
| | | | | |
| | | | | |
| | | | | |
| | | | | |
| | | | | |
| | | | | |
| | | | | |
| | | | | |
| | | | | |

# Cable Information Worksheet

| | | Ref ID: CAB - 9301010001 |
|---|---|---|
| ☐ Type I | Notes: _____ | Originator Name(Print): Josh Levine |
| ☐ Type II | _____ | Signature:_____ |
| ☑ Unshielded Twisted Pair | UTP Throughout | Date Completed:93/08/14 |
| ☐ Other:_____ | _____ | Site Name: XYZ Manufacturing Inc. New York Sales |

## Cabling Checklist

| Cable/Port ID | User Name | Office Location | Passed(Y/N) | Power |
|---|---|---|---|---|
| 1CCT002/2 | Lauren Thompson | 2A10 | ✓ | ✓ |
| 1CCT003/3 | Sarah Nadas | 2A11 | ✓ | ✓ |
| 1CCT004/4 | Teanning Chung | 2A12 | ✓ | ✓ |
| 1CCT001/1 | No User - Work Group Server | 2B1 | ✓ | ✓ |
| | | | | |
| | | | | |
| | | | | |
| | | | | |
| | | | | |
| | | | | |
| | | | | |
| | | | | |
| | | | | |
| | | | | |
| | | | | |
| | | | | |
| | | | | |

Note: For cabling to pass, it must have all the end connectors attached and must be fully functional. For power to pass, there must be a power receptacle present at each desk. It must be capable of handling the anticipated electrical load.

# Change Authorization Form

Ref. ID: CA - 9301010002

Request From: Leslie Shvemar

Department: 3B11 - Cable Engineering

Requestor Signature:

Signing Authority:

## *Change Request*

| Ref. # | Description |
|--------|-------------|
| 001 | Change planned configuration of cable in building sector 7 (See attached recomm.plan) |
| | |
| | |
| | |
| | |
| | |
| | |
| | |
| | |

☐ Change Confirmed          ☑ Change Not Confirmed

Signature:                          Date:

## *Notes*

| Re: Ref. # | Note |
|------------|------|
| 001 | Last minute office relocations. Cable spans too long. Will cause transmission problems. |
| | Recommend switching to cable type 1 and using alternate cable route 24 instead of route 25. |
| | |
| | |
| | |

# Directory Planning Worksheet

User Name/ID: Jean Paul Lauzon/JPLAUZON

Group Name/ID: Accounts Payable/AP

Organization Name/ID: Finance/FIN

Ref ID: DP - 9301010001

Originator Name (Print): Eli Grimson

Signature:

Date Completed:93/08/16

## Root Directory

| Directory Name | WP | SPREADS | INVOICES | INVENTRY | BANKREC | ACCOUNT |
|---|---|---|---|---|---|---|
| Reference # | D1 | D2 | D3 | D4 | D5 | D6 |

| Directory Name | APSOFTW | | | | | |
|---|---|---|---|---|---|---|
| Reference # | D7 | | | | | |

| Directory Name | | | | | | |
|---|---|---|---|---|---|---|
| Reference # | | | | | | |

| Directory Name | | | | | | |
|---|---|---|---|---|---|---|
| Reference # | | | | | | |

| Directory Name | | | | | | |
|---|---|---|---|---|---|---|
| Reference # | | | | | | |

| Directory Name | | | | | | |
|---|---|---|---|---|---|---|
| Reference # | | | | | | |

| Directory Name | | | | | | |
|---|---|---|---|---|---|---|
| Reference # | | | | | | |

# Directory Planning Worksheet

User Name/ID:  Jean Paul Lauzon/JPLAUZON

Group Name/ID:  Accounts Payable/AP

Organization Name/ID:  Finance/FIN

Ref ID: DP - 9301010001

Originator Name (Print):  Eli Grimson

Signature:

Date Completed:93/08/16

*Reference #:*              D1

## Sub-Directories

| Sub-Directory | CORRESP | PERSNNL | ADMIN | FORMLTR | | |
|---|---|---|---|---|---|---|
| Reference # | D1/1 | D1/2 | D1/3 | D1/4 | | |
| Sub-Directory | | | | | | |
| Reference # | | | | | | |
| Sub-Directory | | | | | | |
| Reference # | | | | | | |
| Sub-Directory | | | | | | |
| Reference # | | | | | | |
| Sub-Directory | | | | | | |
| Reference # | | | | | | |
| Sub-Directory | | | | | | |
| Reference # | | | | | | |
| Sub-Directory | | | | | | |
| Reference # | | | | | | |

# End User Profile Worksheet

Name: George Merek     Phone Ext #: 2883     Ref ID: EUP - 9301010001

Location: 2A10     Originator Name (Print): Erin Dawn

Signature:

Job Classification: Management     Date Completed:93/07/21

## Experience

### Workstation Environment

| System Type | Environment | Very Experienced | Somewhat Familiar | Little/No Experience |
|---|---|---|---|---|
| PC386 | DOS | | | ✓ |
| | Microsoft Windows | ✓ | | |
| XYZ Mainframe Term Type 1 | MAINOS | | ✓ | |
| | XYZOFFICE | ✓ | | |
| | | | | |
| | | | | |
| | | | | |
| | | | | |

### Application Software

| Type of Software | Product Name/Version | Experience (Yrs) | Very Experienced | Somewhat Familiar | Little/No Experience |
|---|---|---|---|---|---|
| Word Processor | WordProcess 5.1 | 3.0 | ✓ | | |
| Accounting - Accounts Payable | AcctPayXX.YYY | 1.0 | ✓ | | |
| Groupware - Office Productivity | XYZOfficePRO | 3.0 | ✓ | | |
| | | | | | |
| | | | | | |
| | | | | | |
| | | | | | |

# Equipment Summary
# Worksheet

Ref ID: EQS - 9301010001

Originator Name (Print): Norm Saunders

Signature:

Date Completed: 93/08/17

## Checklist of Equipment

### Computers

| Model Name | CPU Type | Monitor Name | Monitor Type | Count |
|---|---|---|---|---|
| ABC 486XL | 486DX/33 | ABCTrue Screen | VGA | 1 |
| ABC 386EL | 386SX/25 | ABCTrue Screen | VGA | 3 |
| | | | | |
| | | | | |
| | | | | |
| | | | | |

### Printers

| Model Name | Printer Type | Postscript | Compatibility List | Count |
|---|---|---|---|---|
| BrandXModelA | Serial Standard Matrix | | | 1 |
| BrandXModelB | Laser | ✓ | HGII, HGIII | 2 |
| | | | | |
| | | | | |
| | | | | |
| | | | | |

Has the site been cabled: ☐ Yes ☑ No

### Comments

# Equipment Test Sign-off Worksheet

| | | |
|---|---|---|
| ☑ | 24 Hr. Burn-in | Notes:_____ |
| ☑ | Drives Formatted/Tested | _____ |
| ☐ | Hubs Tested | _____ |
| ☑ | Printers Tested | |
| ☑ | Back-up System Tested | _____ |
| ☐ | Other:_____ | _____ |

Ref ID: EQT - 9301010001_____

Originator Name (Print): David Sawh_____

Signature:_____

Date Completed: 93/08/17_____

Device Type: Server_____

Serial #: SN000000002_____

☑ Diagnostics Completed

## Software

| Software Name | Description | Installed/Tested | Drivers Installed | Passed |
|---|---|---|---|---|
| AcctPayXX.YYY | Accounts Payable Master | ✓ | ✓ | ✓ |
| WPXXX.YYY | Word Processing Program | ✓ | ✓ | ✓ |
| | | | | |
| | | | | |
| | | | | |
| | | | | |
| | | | | |
| | | | | |
| | | | | |
| | | | | |
| | | | | |
| | | | | |
| | | | | |
| | | | | |
| | | | | |
| | | | | |
| | | | | |

# Menu Options Worksheet

User Name/ID: Francesca Santos/FSANTOS

Group Name/ID: Accounts Payable/AP

Organization Name/ID: Finance/FIN

Ref ID: MNU - 9301010001

Originator Name (Print): Gino Ruffo

Signature:

Date Completed: 93/08/17

## Main Menu

| Ref. # | Menu Items | Batch File To Execute |
|--------|------------|----------------------|
| 001 | Accounts Payable | ACCXXX.YYY |
| 002 | Word Processing | WPXXX.ZZZ |
| 003 | Electronic Mail | EMXXX.ZZZ |
| 004 | Executive Calendar | CAXXX.ZZZ |
| | | |
| | | |
| | | |

*Sub-Menu:* 001

| Ref. # | Menu Items | Batch File To Execute |
|--------|------------|----------------------|
| 001/1 | Accounts Payable Master File | APMFXX.ZZZ |
| 001/2 | Main Data Entry Module | DEMXX.ZZZ |
| 001/3 | Invoices | INVXX.ZZZ |
| | | |
| | | |
| | | |
| | | |

*Sub-Menu:*

| Ref. # | Menu Items | Batch File To Execute |
|--------|------------|----------------------|
| | | |
| | | |
| | | |
| | | |
| | | |
| | | |
| | | |

# Menu Options Worksheet

User Name/ID:  Francesca Santos/FSANTOS

Group Name/ID:  Accounts Payable/AP

Organization Name/ID:  Finance/FIN

Ref ID: MNU - 9301010001

Originator Name (Print): Gino Ruffo

Signature:

Date Completed: 93/08/17

*Sub-Menu:*

| Ref. # | Menu Items | Batch File To Execute |
|--------|------------|----------------------|
|        |            |                      |
|        |            |                      |
|        |            |                      |
|        |            |                      |
|        |            |                      |
|        |            |                      |

*Sub-Menu:*

| Ref. # | Menu Items | Batch File To Execute |
|--------|------------|----------------------|
|        |            |                      |
|        |            |                      |
|        |            |                      |
|        |            |                      |
|        |            |                      |
|        |            |                      |

*Sub-Menu:*

| Ref. # | Menu Items | Batch File To Execute |
|--------|------------|----------------------|
|        |            |                      |
|        |            |                      |
|        |            |                      |
|        |            |                      |
|        |            |                      |
|        |            |                      |

# Network
# Applications Summary
# Worksheet

Ref ID: NAPP - 9301010001

## *Summary*

| Item | Summary Description |
|---|---|
| AcctPayXX.YY | Main Accounts Payable System. Used By All AP Clerks |
| WordProcess | Standard Word Processor |
| Inventry.YYY | Inventory System |
| | |
| | |
| | |
| | |
| | |

## *Applications Loaded*

| Applications Loaded | Version # | Network Version | User/Group(s) |
|---|---|---|---|
| AcctPayXX.YYY | 1.0 | ✓ | Accounts Payable, Accounting |
| WordProcess | 5.1 | ✓ | All |
| Inventry.YYY | 2.1 | ✓ | Finance |
| | | | |
| | | | |
| | | | |
| | | | |
| | | | |

Completed By: Aris Economopolis          On Date:93/08/17

# Network Maintenance Log

Ref ID: MTC - <u>9301010001</u>

| | | | |
|---|---|---|---|
| ☐ | System Login Script | ☐ | Normal/Routine |
| ☑ | User Login Script | ☑ | Trouble Resolution |
| ☐ | Gateways, Modems | | |
| ☐ | Directory Structure(s) | | |

Nature of Problem: <u>User could not log in to system</u>

☐ Start-up Files/Configuration

☐ Workstations

☐ Bridges/Routers

☐ Software Upgrades

☐ NLM, Vaps, etc.

☐ _____

☐ _____

☐ _____

☐ _____

*Nature of Changes*

| Ref. # | Description |
|---|---|
| 001 | User could not log in to main server. Problem due to corrupt login script file. |
| | Rebuilt file and tested. Everything is now fine. |
| | |
| | |
| | |
| | |
| | |
| | |
| | |

Changed By: <u>Janet Lee</u>          On Date:<u>93/08/17</u>

Authorization:_____          Date:<u>93/08/17</u>

# Operating System Configuration Worksheet

☑ Novell Netware   Version: 3.2   Server Name:SERVER1   Ref ID: NOS - 9301010003

☐ Banyan Vines   _____   Workstation ID:_____   Originator Name (Print): Pascale Ashworth

☐ Microsoft LAN Manager   _____   Network Address:1   Signature:_____

☐ Other:_____   _____   Communications Buffers: 55   Date Completed:93/12/31

## Resource Sets

*Communications/LAN Interface Boards*

| LAN ID | Name/Description | Option # | Interrupt IRQ | I/O Base Address | DMA | Network Address |
|--------|------------------|----------|---------------|------------------|-----|-----------------|
| A | ABCFastcardE-Net 32Bit | 1 | 2 | 2E0 | 2 | 1 |
| | | | | | | |
| | | | | | | |
| | | | | | | |
| | | | | | | |

*Hard Disk Channel Drives*

| Chan # | Name/Description | Option # | Interrupt IRQ | I/O Base Address | DMA | Notes |
|--------|------------------|----------|---------------|------------------|-----|-------|
| 1 | Quantum-X | 2 | 14 | 1F0 | | |
| | | | | | | |
| | | | | | | |
| | | | | | | |
| | | | | | | |

*Other:_____   Optical Disk Drive_____*

| Ref. # | Name/Description | Option # | Interrupt IRQ | I/O Base Address | DMA | Notes |
|--------|------------------|----------|---------------|------------------|-----|-------|
| 2 | OPTICOM-A | 0 | | D0001 | | Used For Clip Art |
| | | | | | | |
| | | | | | | |
| | | | | | | |
| | | | | | | |

# Operating System Configuration Worksheet

Ref ID: NOS - <u>9301010003</u>

Originator Name (Print): <u>Pascale Ashworth</u>

Signature:_____

Date Completed:<u>93/12/31</u>

## Resource Sets

*Serial Printer Configurations*

| Port | Serial #/Name | Printer Type | Baud Rate | Word Size | Stop Bits | Parity | xon /xoff | Poll | Int | Queue Name | Spool # |
|------|---------------|--------------|-----------|-----------|-----------|--------|-----------|------|-----|------------|---------|
| 1 | SN111111/BrandXModel | Standard | 9600 | 7 | 7 | off | | 15 sec | 4 | PRN1 | 5 |
| | | | | | | | | | | | |
| | | | | | | | | | | | |
| | | | | | | | | | | | |
| | | | | | | | | | | | |
| | | | | | | | | | | | |

*Parallel Printer Configurations*

| Port | Serial #/Name | Printer Type | Poll | Interrupt | Queue Name | Spool # |
|------|---------------|--------------|------|-----------|------------|---------|
| 2 | SN11111123/BrandX-XA | Postscript | 15 sec | 7 | PRN2 | 4 |
| | | | | | | |
| | | | | | | |
| | | | | | | |
| | | | | | | |
| | | | | | | |

*Volume Information*

| Volume Name | Directory Cached(Y/N) | # of Directory Entries | Size (Mb) | Notes |
|-------------|----------------------|------------------------|-----------|-------|
| ACCVOL | No | 5 | 255 | Accounting Information |
| SYS 1 | Yes | 20 | 500 | Main |
| | | | | |
| | | | | |
| | | | | |
| | | | | |
| | | | | |

# Project Status
# Report

Project ID: 930001-00

Project Name: N.Y. Sales Office LAN

Client Name: Sales Dept.

Project Leader: Bob Myers

Ref ID: PSR - 9301010001

Originator Name (Print): Bob Myers

Signature:

Date Completed:93/08/20

## *Accomplished This Period*

Finished cabling floors 1 to 3. Terminating jacks and wall outlets are completed.

## *Unresolved Problems Or Obstacles*

No problems to report this week.

## *Objectives For Next Period*

Finish cabling floor 4 and 5.

*Status Update - For Period Ending: (YY/MM/DD):*          93/08/20

| Task ID | Task Name | Start Date | % Complete | Est. Date for Completion | Notes |
|---------|-----------|------------|------------|--------------------------|-------|
| 001 | Install Cabling | 93/08/1 | 50% | 93/08/30 | Don't expect any problems |
|  |  |  |  |  |  |
|  |  |  |  |  |  |
|  |  |  |  |  |  |
|  |  |  |  |  |  |

# Prototyping Log

Ref ID: PTYP - 9301010002

Originator Name (Print): Jonathon Hirsh

Signature:

Date Completed: 93/08/17

## *Description and Purpose*

Vendor has new product called SuperWidgetABC that they say is in the final stages of becoming commercially available. It is not yet in production. We want to test it in our lab to verify that it performs to specification.

## *Methodology*

Assemble product in lab. Connect SuperWidgetABC to a server. Monitor the data packets being sent and the performance impacts on the server. Monitor performance on the LAN segment and on the server itself. Should this test prove that the performance decrease is not greater than .25 milliseconds, it will be considered a success.

## *Results/Action Items*

Performance decrease was .1 milliseconds. Successful evaluation. Recommend using it in the field.

Signing Authority: Date Approved: 93/08/17

# Security Profile Worksheet

Ref ID: SEC - <u>9301010001</u>

Originator Name (Print):<u>Gian Brandolisio</u>

Signature:_____

Owner Name

User Name: <u>Lauren Eden</u>

Date Completed:<u>93/08/17</u>

Group Name:_____

Owner Signature:_____

Organization Name: <u>H.Q. Marketing</u>

Date:<u>93/08/17</u>

## Effective Rights

### *Access Given To - Delegate Name*

| *Directory Path* | User Name | Group Name | Organization Name | Access Rights | Notes |
|---|---|---|---|---|---|
| **C:\SAMPLE\DATA\paymaster** | | **H.Q. Finance** | | **RWOM** | **Needed For Month-End** |
| G:\FORECASTS | Scott Taylor | Forecasting | Finance | R | Data for revenue project'ns |
| G:\PRODINFO | | Major Accts | Sales | R | Product info for sales staff |
| G:\FEEDBACK | | Major Accts | Sales | RW | Sales feedback for mktg |
| G:\SFTWRE\CONFIGS | | | Sales | ROFX | Product Pricing Programs |
| | | | | | |
| | | | | | |
| | | | | | |
| | | | | | |
| | | | | | |
| | | | | | |
| | | | | | |
| | | | | | |
| | | | | | |
| | | | | | |
| | | | | | |
| | | | | | |
| | | | | | |

| | | | |
|---|---|---|---|
| R=Read Only | D=Delete | E=Erase | ____ = _____ |
| W=Write Only | S=Search | F=File Scan | ____ = _____ |
| O=Open Only | P=Parental | A=Access Control | ____ = _____ |
| C=Create | M=Modify | X=Execute | ____ = _____ |

# Server Configuration Worksheet

Ref ID: SVR - _____ 93010001 _____

Originator Name (Print): _____ Dan Grant _____

Signature: _____

Date Completed: _____ 94/07/07 _____

## Processor and Bus Type

☐ 80286 _____ ☐ 80386 _____ ☑ 80486 DX33 ☐ Other:_____

☑ ISA ☐ EISA ☐ MCA ☐ Other:_____ Serial Number: ___ SN000000002 ___

## Disk Storage Devices

☑ Floppy (1.2m 5.25In) ☑ Hard Drive 1 _500Mb_ Space Left -1 _300Mb_ ☑ Mirror ☑ Duplexed

☑ Floppy (1.44m 3.5In) ☑ Hard Drive 2_____ Space Left -2_____ ☐ Mirror ☐ Duplexed

☐ Floppy (360kb 5.25In)

☐ Floppy (720Kb 3.5In)     Drive Type

☐ IDE ☐ MFM ☑ ESDI ☐ RRL ☐ Other:_____

## Memory

☑ Base RAM Size _640K_

☑ Extended _____ 7Mb _____ ☑ Expanded_____

## Interfaces

☑ Serial ___ 3 ___ ☑ Parallel ___ 3 ___ ☐ SCSI_____ ☐ Other:_____

## Graphics Card/Monitor Type

☑ VGA Color ☐ SVGA _____ ☐ Other:_____ Resolution _1024_ X _768_    ☑ Interlaced

☐ Non-interlaced

## Network Interface Card

☐ 8 Bit ☑ 16 Bit ☐ 32 Bit

☐ Token Ring 4Mb ☐ Token Ring 16Mb ☐ Arcnet ☑ Ethernet ☐ Other:_____

Base Address _____ C000 _____ DMA _____ 3 _____ Node Address _2_ IRQ _____ 3 _____

## UPS

☑ Installed ☐ Not Installed

☐ 550VA ☐ 1000VA ☑ 1500V ☐ Other:_____

## Warranty

Vendor: _ABC Computers Inc._      Expiry Date: ____ 94/12/31 ____

# Team Contacts Worksheet

Ref ID: TM - TCW9301010001

Project Name: NYSALESBRANCHLAN

Project ID: 930001-00

Organization Name: IT Support

Key Contact: Bob Esbin

Phone #: AAA-BBBB

## Participant Members

| Name | Title | Office Location | Phone # | Role(s) |
|------|-------|-----------------|---------|---------|
| George Nadas | Mgr. IT Support | NY Head Office | AAA-BBBB | Project Leader |
| Josh Rosenberg | Sr. Business Consultant,HQ.Systems | NY Head Office | AAA-BBBB | Technology Adv. |
| Ariel Winslow | Administrative Assistant | NY Head Office | AAA-BBBB | Project Admin. |
| Gino Ruffo | Installation Specialist, IT Support | NY Head Office | AAA-BBBB | Install. Specialist |
| Scott Maavara | Training Manager, HQ Info Resources | NY Head Office | AAA-BBBB | Trainer |
| | | | | |
| | | | | |
| | | | | |
| | | | | |
| | | | | |
| | | | | |
| | | | | |
| | | | | |
| | | | | |

## Supporting Groups

| Group Name | Key Contacts | Phone # | Role(s) | Notes |
|------------|--------------|---------|---------|-------|
| HQ Engineering | Doug Hylton | 555-1212 | Tech. Design | Reports to Mike |
| Cable Systems Design Inc. | Ian Hindsmith | 555-XXXX | Cable Installer | On contract |
| Able Telecom Inc. | Guy Marchand | 416-555-1212 | Phone Co. | Sales rep. |
| | | | | |
| | | | | |
| | | | | |
| | | | | |

# Wiring Closet Information
# Worksheet

**CLOSET ID/LOCATION**   Floor 3 North East Wall

Ref ID: WC - 9301010001

Originator Name (Print): Brian Collie

Signature:_____

Date Completed:93/08/17

Existing

☐ Type I          Note _____

☐ Type II                  _____

☑ Unshielded Twisted Pair    _____

☐ Other_____          _____

Site Name: XYZ Manufacturing NY Sales

Installer:_Hannah Oatley

<u>Environmental Specifications</u>

Closet Dimensions      Length  3 m          Width  3 m            Height  3.7 m

Number of Receptacles: 5

Number of Shelves: 10

Ambient Closet Temperature: 23        Degrees  ☑ Centigrade   ☐ Fahrenheit

Ventilation      ☑ Fan          ☐ Ventilation Slots

## *Notes*

Building only 2 years old. Closets set up for UTP cable. Other LANs present in building. Clean throughout. Door is not secure.

- Recommend door replacement with steel door.
- Already wired with Unshielded Twisted Pair

# Work Group Information Worksheet

Ref ID: WI - 9301010001
Originator Name (Print): Ann Bigcanoe
Signature: _____
Date Completed:93/08/17

User Group: Accounts Payable
Function: Data Entry
Supervisor Name: Matt McCarthy
Phone #: 111-222-3333

Department Name: Finance
Dept. #/Location: 1234/2A

## Workstations and Servers

| System Type | Serial Number | Location | Hard Disk Capacity(Mb) | FDD | Total Memory | Monitor Type | Port ID | Cable Connection | Cable Type | Attached Printer Ser.# | Modem | Main Applications Loaded |
|---|---|---|---|---|---|---|---|---|---|---|---|---|
| PC486/33 | SN000000002 SN00000000002 | 2B1 | 470 | 3.5,5.2 | 8Mb | VGA | 1 | 1CCT001 | UTP | SN111112 SN11111 | SYN19.2 ASYN240 | AcctPayXX.YYY, Inventry.YYY |
| PC386/25 | SN0000000000 | 2A10 | 150 | 3.5,5.2 | 4Mb | VGA | 2 | 1CCT002 | UTP | None | None | App1, App2, App3... |
| PC386/25 | SN0000000000 | 2A11 | 150 | 3.5,5.2 | 4Mb | VGA | 3 | 1CCT003 | UTP | None | None | App1, App2, App3... |
| PC386/25 | SN0000000000 | 2A12 | 150 | 3.5,5.2 | 4Mbu | VGA | 4 | 1CCT004 | UTP | None | None | App1, App2, App3... |
| | | | | | | | | | | | | |
| | | | | | | | | | | | | |

## Printers

| Printer Type | Name/Model | Emulation(s) | Serial # | Shared /Ntwk | No. of Users | Memory (Mb) | No. Trays | Tray Types |
|---|---|---|---|---|---|---|---|---|
| Postscript | BrandXModelB | | SN1111123 | ✓ | 3 | 4 | 2 | Letter, Legal |
| Serial Standard | BrandXModelA | | SN11111 | ✓ | 3 | | 0 | Continuous Feed Only |
| | | | | | | | | |

## Interest Group(s)

| Dept. Name | Group Name | Location |
|---|---|---|
| Finance | Acc.Receiv. | 2C |
| Finance | Payments | 2D |
| Sales | Major Accts. | 5A |
| Sales | Gen. Accts. | 5B |

# Workstation Configuration Worksheet

Ref ID: SVR - _____9301010001_____
Originator Name (Print):___Raffi Anwar___
Signature:_____
Date Completed:_____94/07/07_____

## Processor and Bus Type

☐ 80286 ____ ✔ 80386 DX/33 ☐ 80486 ____ ☐ Other:_____

✔ ISA ☐ EISA ☐ MCA ☐ Other:_____ Serial Number:__SN00000000000__

## Disk Storage Devices

☐ Floppy (1.2m 5.25In) ✔ Hard Drive 1 150 Mb Space Left -1__75Mb__
✔ Floppy (1.44m 3.5In) ☐ Hard Drive 2_____ Space Left -2_____
☐ Floppy (360kb 5.25In) Drive Type
☐ Floppy (720Kb 3.5In) ☐ IDE ☐ MFM ✔ ESDI ☐ RRL ☐ Other:_____

## Memory

✔ Base RAM Size_640K_
✔ Extended____3Mb____ ☐ Expanded_____

## Interfaces

✔ Serial__2____ ✔ Parallel__1__ ☐ SCSI____ ☐ Other:_____

## Graphics Card/Monitor Type

✔ VGA Color ☐ SVGA _____ ☐ Other:_____ Resolution 640_ X 480_ ☐ Interlaced
✔ Non-interlaced

## Network Interface Card

☐ 8 Bit ✔ 16 Bit ☐ 32 Bit
☐ Token Ring 4Mb ☐ Token Ring 16Mb ☐ Arcnet ✔ Ethernet ☐ Other:_____
Base Address____C000____ DMA____3____ Node Address__2__ IRQ____3____

## UPS

✔ Installed ☐ Not Installed
☐ 550VA ✔ 1000VA ☐ 1500V ☐ Other:_____

## Warranty

Vendor:__ABC Computers Inc.__ Expiry Date:____94/12/31____

# GLOSSARY

# GLOSSARY

This glossary contains not only the technical terminology found throughout the book, but also numerous terms which are not used but which you may encounter in the course of the implementation. All terms boldfaced within the definitions are also defined in the Glossary.

**Access method**: A set of rules used by network software and hardware to determine which workstation will be next to use the LAN, as well as to direct LAN traffic. Examples of access methods are **token passing** and **carrier-sense multiple access with collision detection**.

**Account set-up worksheet**: A form showing a user's, group's, or organization's name; account default settings; and the applications access section.

**Address**: A set of numbers identifying the location of a node or device on a network. Each node on a network must have a unique address.

**American Standard Code for Information Interchange (ASCII)**: A standard eight-bit character code for data transfer among computing devices, data communication systems, and associated equipment. (Seven of the eight bits are used for information, one for parity check.)

**Application pilot**: A limited-scale test procedure for unproven information technology, generally used during the planning and design phase of the STEPS process.

**Application pilot summary report**: A document which consolidates all application pilot results and management's comments on them.

**Applications details worksheet**: A form which establishes the nature of the commercially available and the custom-developed applications currently used in a given environment.

**ASCII**: See **American Standard Code for Information Interchange**.

**Asynchronous**: Refers to a communications method in which each character is independently transmitted, with no relationship to another.

**Asynchronous protocol**: A simple protocol over a communications line, often referred to as a start-stop or an X.28.

**Audit trail**: In the context of a communications network, a detailed list of information (all call connections, disconnections, errors, and malfunctions) identified and stored by the network management system. In the context of the STEPS process, the signed documentation generated at various points in order to maintain project tracking and accountability.

**Backbone network**: An organization's main network; generally consists of high-speed facilities.

**Back-up log**: A document in which all information about the timing and nature of back-ups is recorded on a routine basis.

**Baseband**: An electrical signaling technique used to transmit information by means of unmodulated signals. The entire frequency range of the channel is used during transmission. See also **broadband**.

**Batch communications**: A form of data communication in which a facility collects information over time and submits it to a host computer for processing according to a regular schedule. In batch communications, large amounts of information are typically transmitted at scheduled intervals.

**Bridge**: Equipment that connects LANs, permitting communication between devices on them, thus allowing network traffic to traverse similar LANs or protocol types along its path.

**Broadband**: An electrical signaling technique used to transmit information by means of modulated signals. Broadband networks typically divide the total bandwidth of the communication channel into multiple subchannels which use different frequencies. The subchannels may allow video, voice, and data transmission simultaneously. See also **baseband**.

**Burn-in**: A method for testing computer-related hardware in which the device being checked is left running for a specified period — usually 24 hours — while connected to special diagnostic gear.

**Business case**: The examination of costs versus anticipated benefits; done before any proposed solution is implemented. See also **cost-benefit analysis**.

**Bus topology**: A topology characterized by a long span of cable, with each node attached serially. See also **topology**.

**Cable information worksheet**: A form on which all existing types of cable, their locations and terminations, and cable testing results are noted.

**Carrier-sense multiple access with collision detection (CSMA /CD)**: An access method that allows many nodes or devices to share a single communication channel. If more than one node attempts to transmit at a given moment, the signals collide and are then retransmitted. Ethernet uses this access method, which is often referred to as IEEE 802.3.

**CCITT**: See **Comité Consultatif International Télégraphique et Téléphonique**.

**Champion**: A non-systems person who demonstrates greater-than-average interest in and aptitude for the use of computer tools.

**Change authorization form**: A document listing alterations to approved plans; a key project audit item. Each change request is described on the form and circulated to a signing authority for approval.

**Circuit**: A communication path between two devices which allows the exchange of information. Equivalent to **connection** and **session**.

**Coaxial cable**: A transmission medium containing a central conductor which carries information signals and an outer conductor (electrostatic shielding) which acts as a ground.

**Collision detection**: See **Carrier-sense multiple access with collision detection (CSMA /CD)**.

**Comité Consultatif International Télégraphique et Téléphonique (CCITT)**: An international advisory committee set up under United Nations sponsorship to oversee and recommend standards for international communications. (French for International Telegraph and Telephone Consultation Committee.)

**Commercial applications details worksheet**: A form which establishes the nature of the commercially available applications currently used in a given environment. Used in combination with the **custom applications details worksheet**.

**Configuration**: In the context of this book, taking off-the-shelf hardware or software and, by using its self-contained options and usage parameters, tailoring it to one's own use.

**Connection**: A communication path between two devices which allows the exchange of information. Equivalent to **circuit** and **session**.

**Cost-benefit analysis**: The examination of costs versus anticipated benefits; done before any proposed solution is implemented. See also **business case**.

**CRC**: See **cyclical redundancy check**.

**CSMA /CD**: See **Carrier-sense multiple access with collision detection**.

**Custom applications details worksheet**: A form which establishes the nature of the custom-developed applications currently used in a given environment. Used in combination with the **commercial applications details worksheet**.

**Cyclical redundancy check (CRC)**: A method of detecting errors in a message by performing a mathematical calculation on the bits in the message, then sending the result of the calculation along with the message. The receiving network station performs the same calculation on the message, then checks its result against the result it received. If the results do not match, the receiving end asks the sending end to send the entire message again.

**Datagram**: A transmission method in which sections of a message are transmitted in scattered sequence; their proper order is re-established by the receiving workstation.

**Detailed pilot specification document**: A description of the pilot system's features and functionality, its detailed technical design specifications and how it will mesh with the environment, together with purchasing information for pilot system hardware and software.

**Directory planning worksheet**: A form used to define the directory structures of both workstations and servers at the user, group, and organizational levels.

**Disk drive mapping:** A technique which involves assigning a disk drive letter, such as G:, to a particular directory path. For example, G: could be assigned to F:\PAYABLES, forming a logical association. When G: is referred to, the system automatically refers to F:\PAYABLES.

**Driver**: Software which allows either system operating software or user applications software to use a particular piece of equipment. For example, word processor software comes on diskettes which also contain drivers that permit the use of any number of types of printers.

**Equipment summary worksheet**: A form which provides a summary of equipment inventory.

**Equipment test sign-off worksheet**: A form used to report the successful testing of both hardware and software.

**Ethernet**: A data link protocol that uses baseband signaling at 10 Mbps. It is used as the underlying transport vehicle for many LANS and is considered by many to be the predominant local area network standard.

**Exposure:** In the context of this book, exposure is discussed in terms of exposure to **risk**, and has a range of elements: how capable one is of determining who requires access to what information; how easy it is to access the network from the outside; and the ability to trace an intrusion and block further occurrences.

**FDDI**: See **fibre distributed data interface**.

**FEP**: See **front-end processor**.

**Fibre distributed data interface (FDDI)**: A network standard based on dual counter-rotating 100 Mbps token rings. There are two separate rings, with information packets in one ring travelling in the opposite direction to the information packets in the other ring. FDDI uses the token passing access method. See also **access method, packet, token passing**, and **token ring**.

**Flow control**: The hardware or software mechanisms employed in data communications to turn transmission off and on when the receiving workstation is unable to store the data it is receiving.

**Formal instruction**: A training approach which requires an instructor and has an identifiable structure designed to develop an individual's occupational skills. It may be carried out on the job or in a classroom setting, on or off site, during or after work hours.

**Front-end processor**: A device typically attached to IBM mainframe computers. Its functions include network routing and traffic concentration for the host.

**Full back-up**: A back-up of this sort involves saving all selected files simultaneously. Restoring the information involves loading the last full back-up and selecting the files to be restored — if necessary, the entire disk.

**Functional requirements specification document**: A document which identifies and defines precise functional business needs, and also details the proposed system's features and functionality requirements. See also **functional requirements specification outline**.

**Functional requirements specification outline**: A document which provides a framework for detailing what an organization needs a new system to do, in terms of the functional requirements of the business. Each item is included to guarantee that corporate objectives, business units' specific objectives, and functional requirements relating to the system are all met. See also **functional requirements specification document**.

**Gantt chart**: A chart used to show project schedules and tracking. Its left-hand column contains a list of tasks. The chart also contains a graphic of horizontal bars, and an overhead calendar. The bars illustrate the tasks planned or scheduled, or actual progress over time.

**Gateway**: A computing device and its software which permit two networks using dissimilar protocols to communicate with one another.

**Incremental back-up**: In this sort of back-up, only those files which have been created, copied, or modified since the last back-up — whether full or incremental — are saved.

**Informal training**: A form of instruction provided by a more experienced fellow worker or a supervisor of the trainee, and always done on the job during normal hours.

**International Standards Organization (ISO)**: An international standards group composed of co-operating industries.

**ISO**: See **International Standards Organization**.

**LAN**: See **local area network**.

**Local area network (LAN)**: A system formed by physically connecting several computers and related equipment, so that all the devices can communicate with one another without requiring a central processor. Its purpose is to allow the sharing of common resources such as printers, databases, input/output devices, and data storage devices. See also **wide area network (WAN)**.

**Menu options worksheet**: A form on which to define the hierarchy of menus, which help the user select and access computer applications and resources.

**Needs analysis study**: An exercise whose purpose is to research organizational needs and identify appropriate opportunities for change. A needs analysis study should always be consistent with the corporate information technology plan.

**Need-to-know rule**: A user should have access only to the information that he or she actually requires.

**Network applications summary worksheet**: A form showing all the shared network applications which reside on a server.

**Network device**: A point in a network where service is provided or used, or communication channels are interconnected. Equivalent to **node** and **station device**.

**Network interface card (NIC)**: A circuit card which is inserted into the network devices or nodes, making possible their physical attachment to the network.

**Network maintenance log**: A document in which system upgrades and solutions to problems are recorded for reference and audit purposes. A single log or form is used for each maintenance item.

**Network management**: The responsibility for overseeing and maintaining a network. Network management functions include network configuration, the monitoring of performance, security maintenance, and fault detection.

**Network overview schematic**: A high-level blueprint of the proposed layout for a given work environment; provides a conceptual look at the types and locations of all major LAN components and their means of interconnection.

**NIC**: See **network interface card**.

**Node**: A point in a network where service is provided or used, or communication channels are interconnected. Equivalent to **station device** and **network device**.

**Open systems interconnection (OSI)**: A seven-layer communication model defined by the International Standards Organization (ISO) which provides a comprehensive structure for reliable, effective data communication.

**Operating system configuration worksheet**: A form on which the parameters for an operating system are defined.

**Packet**: A block of data organized according to a predefined format for handling by a network.

**Packet assembler and disassembler (PAD)**: A self-contained box, a PC card, and/or software which resides in a computer. Its purpose is to provide both a line speed and a protocol interface for non-X.25 computing devices, allowing them to communicate over an X.25 network.

**Packet switching**: A network designed to carry and route data in the form of packets.

**PAD**: See **packet assembler and disassembler**.

**PDN**: See **public data network**.

**PERT chart**: A program evaluation and review technique chart giving a graphic representation of interrelated events and the order in which they occur. Pert charts are generally used to show the relationship among interdependent events depicted as text enclosed in boxes. Often referred to as a process chart.

**Pre-configuration**: The processes of installing hardware and configuring software, before they are actually needed. See also **configuration**.

**Project status report**: A document used by the project team to track the progress of the implementation, showing objectives, accomplishments, problem areas, and a project task status list.

**Protocol**: A set of guidelines and procedures that permit the orderly exchange of information within and across a network. They normally encompass and govern the format, timing, sequencing, and error control for the exchange.

**Prototyping**: The task of building a model in a controlled setting to see whether it works as anticipated. All new non-standard products should be examined and compared to organizational standards in this manner before implementation, as should special assemblies or configurations.

**Prototyping log**: A document, used for audit purposes, in which precise descriptions of all testing methods, evaluation criteria, and equipment specifications for a prototype are recorded.

**Public data network (PDN)**: A network providing data transmission services to the public, typically by using packet switching technology.

**Request for information (RFI)**: A formal request for specific information relating to products, support, and services.

**Request for proposal (RFP)**: A formal request for a detailed proposal, including firm pricing, to address the specific requirements at hand.

**Request for quotation (RFQ)**: A formal request for pricing related to products, support, and services.

**RFI**: See **request for information**.

**RFP**: See **request for proposal**.

**RFQ**: See **request for quotation**.

**Rights mask:** A filtering system used to define access privileges for information resources ranging from computer programs to databases.

**Ring topology**: A topology so named because of the physical ring formed by the transmission medium. Devices in it are connected to one another in a serial fashion, like links in a chain, to form a ring. See also **token ring** and **topology**.

**Risk**: In the context of LAN security, the possibility of loss, theft, or corruption of the information on a network.

**Router**: A device normally consisting of both hardware and software whose purpose is to route information (information packets) from one LAN to another. The use of a router allows network traffic to traverse dissimilar LAN or protocol types along its path.

**SCSI**: See **small computer system interface**.

**SDLC**: See **synchronous data link control**.

**Security profile worksheet**: A form used to assign access privileges to specific users and interest groups.

**Server**: In its most common form, a high-capacity PC with a network operating system running in server configuration mode; comprised of both hardware and software. Designed for use by a given community of users, it gives them the capability to share printers, hard disks, tape back-up drives, and other devices resident with the server. It also provides communication services such as E-mail, as well as communications access to remote applications.

**Server configuration worksheet**: A form that records details about the servers in a system, including type of processor, type of disk storage, memory, and interfaces.

**Session**: A communication path between two devices which allows the exchange of information. Equivalent to **circuit** and **connection**.

**SIR**: See **site inspection report**.

**Site inspection report (SIR)**: A compilation of various STEPS: Forms and other documents describing an organization's current work environment in both functional and physical terms.

**Site upgrade requirements report (SURR)**: A compilation of various STEPS: Forms and other documents detailing all the physical site requirements that must be addressed before installation, the costs involved, and target dates for completion of the work.

**Small computer system interface (SCSI)**: A relatively high-performance interface typically used between a storage resource, such as a tape drive, and a computer system. Also used to connect a printer to a computer.

**SSR**: See **system solution report**.

**Star topology**: A topology with a central network hub which branches out to remote workstations or servers. Its architecture is much like a telephone system with its central controller branching out to each telephone set. A star network is characterized by point-to-point communications. See also **topology**.

**Station device**: A point in a network where service is provided or used, or communication channels are interconnected. Equivalent to **network device** and **node**.

**Subnet**: A portion of a network which is partitioned by a router.

**SURR**: See **site upgrade requirements report**.

**Switching**: A technology which dynamically routes multiple packets of information from source to destination.

**Synchronous data link control (SDLC)**: A bit-oriented protocol that transmits data in frames; used in an IBM systems network architecture (SNA) to transmit data over a communication link.

**Sysgen:** See **system generation**.

**System generation**: The process of configuring or reconfiguring system-related programs. The term is commonly used in speaking of the initial set-up and configuration of LAN operating system software.

**System prototyping**: The task of building a model of a system. See also **prototyping**.

**System solution report (SSR)**: A compilation of STEPS: Forms and other documents containing detailed descriptive information and specifications for a proposed design solution and its implementation.

**T1 carrier**: A digital transmission system which sends information at 1.544 Mbps; can transmit both voice and data. Equivalent to **T1 link**.

**T1 link**: A digital transmission system which sends information at 1.544 Mbps; can transmit both voice and data. Equivalent to **T1 carrier**.

**TCP / IP**: See **transmission control protocol / internet protocol**.

**Team contacts worksheet**: A document that identifies all members of the project team and supporting resource people, and gives their telephone numbers.

**Token passing**: An access method in which one or more empty packets circulate around a ring. When a station has something to send, it finds the first available empty packet or token, replaces it with a packet containing data, and sends it along its path, where it is read and retransmitted if it has not reached its final destination address. A packet makes a full rotation on the ring until it reaches its destination, which then marks the packet as delivered and sends it back to the source station. When the source packet retrieves the packet, it marks it as empty and sends it back onto the ring for use by others. See also **access method**, **packet**, and **token ring**.

**Token ring**: A technology developed by IBM which uses the ring topology and token passing access method to control traffic on a LAN. See also **access method** and **token passing**.

**Topology**: The physical layout of workstations and other peripheral devices connected to a network; may be classified into three basic types: **star topology**, **ring topology**, and **bus topology**.

**Transmission control protocol / Internet protocol (TCP / IP)**: A set of networking standards commonly used over Ethernet or X.25 networks which defines high-level protocols such as Telnet (terminal connection), FTP (file transfer), and SMTP (electronic mail). Originally developed by the US government, TCP / IP is supported today by many equipment manufacturers.

**Trouble ticket**: A mechanism for tracking a network problem from identification through resolution.

**Twisted pair**: A type of wiring commonly used for telephone installations which takes two forms: shielded twisted pair and unshielded twisted pair. Most standard networks, such as Ethernet and token ring, can use this type of cable. The 10BASE-T standard for Ethernet transmission uses twisted pair wiring.

**Uninterrupted power supply (UPS)**: A battery back-up normally used to support the critical elements of a network. A server should be on an uninterrupted power supply.

**UPS**: See **uninterrupted power supply**.

**WAN**: See **wide area network**.

**Wide area network (WAN)**: A system which serves an area larger than that served by a local area network. The area may consist of two adjacent buildings or thousands of kilometres. A WAN may be comprised of both public and private network facilities. See also **local area network**.

**Wiring closet information worksheet**: A form on which each wiring closet is described in terms of both the types of cables and environmental conditions.

**Work group information worksheet**: A form which gives a high-level view of all equipment and configurations within a given work group, looking at such details as type of PC, overall disk capacity, type of printer, and so on.

**Workstation**: A personal computer.

**Workstation configuration worksheet**: A form which gives information on the "nuts and bolts" of the equipment, looking at such internal details as the processor type, memory, and capacity of disk drives.

**X.25**: A CCITT standard that defines the communications protocol used in public or private packet switching networks, which are often referred to as X.25 networks.

**X.75**: The CCITT recommendation for packet network interworking. X.75 supports both communications between adjacent networks and communications through transit networks.

**Order Your Copy of STEPS: Tools On Disk**

# STEPS FOR IMPLEMENTING LOCAL AREA NETWORKS
## A BUSINESS GUIDE

### Register and order your STEPS: Tools Special Offers.

STEPS: Tools on disk includes all STEPS: Forms and STEPS: Process Charts in the book.
Complete the registration and order form below, printing your name and address.
If ordering, please include method of payment and signature. Mail these forms to:

Attention STEPS: Tools
CAUCHI DENNISON & ASSOCIATES INC.
367 Spadina Road
Toronto, Ontario
CANADA
M5P 2V7

Or, for faster service across North America, fax to: **1-416-485-6566**
(Please use black ink to fax)

## REGISTRATION FORM

☐ **Register Me Today**... Keep me posted for updates and qualify me for the special product promotions outlined below and on the facing page.

Name:_____

Title:_____

Company:_____

*Street:_____

City: _____  State/Province:_____

Zip/Postal Code:_____  Country:_____

Area Code and Phone No.:_____  Fax No.:_____

*Street address only. Delivery cannot be made to a P.O. Box.

## METHOD OF PAYMENT ☐ VISA ☐ Master Card ☐ AMEX

Card No.:_____

Card Holder Name:_____

Expiry Date:_____

Signature:_____

## ORDER FORM

| | Send Information Only | Diskette Size 3.5" | Diskette Size 5.25" | List Price | STEPS: Special Price | Quantity | Amount |
|---|---|---|---|---|---|---|---|
| STEPS: Tools--Process Charts and Forms--Printable Graphic Files (Microsoft Windows version 3.1 Print Files and .EPS Files) | | | | $100 US $120 CDN | $50 US $60 CDN | | |
| STEPS: Tools--Project Templates for Microsoft Project version 3.0 for Windows (.MPP Files) and Electronic Forms for DELRINA PerForm PRO Plus (.FRP Files) | | | | $398 US $478 CDN | $199 US $239 CDN | | |
| | | | | | Sub total | | |
| | | | | Shipping & Handling add $10 in Canada / $30 in US | | | |
| | | | | Add applicable provincial or state sales tax & GST in Canada | | | |
| | | | | | Total of order | | |

Special offer available only to validated owners of *STEPS FOR IMPLEMENTING LOCAL AREA NETWORKS*.
See registration instructions.

STEPS: Tools is a trademark of Cauchi Dennison & Associates Inc.

# STEPS FOR IMPLEMENTING LOCAL AREA NETWORKS
## A BUSINESS GUIDE

These special software discount offers are available only to owners of
***STEPS FOR IMPLEMENTING LOCAL AREA NETWORKS***.

## MICROSOFT ® Project 3.0 For Windows ™
***Special Offer*** $199 US ($249 in Canada) Suggested Retail Price $695 US

To order, call Microsoft direct...and ask for the "STEPS: For LANs $199 Special Offer"

*In the US, call* **1-800-426-9400**

*In Canada, call* **1-800-563-9048**

Offer good only direct from Microsoft, until September 31, 1993, or while supplies last.
When ordering, inquire about specific system requirements. The first copy of Microsoft Project is $199 US; additional
copies are $695 US. All prices are exclusive of applicable sales tax and shipping and handling charges.

● ● ● ● ● ● ● ● ● ● ● ● ● ● ● ● ● ● ● ● ● ● ● ● ● ● ● ● ● ● ● ● ● ● ● ● ● ● ● ● ● ● ● ● ● ● ● ● ● ● ● ● ● ● ●

## DELRINA PerForm PRO Plus
***Special Offer*** $199 US ($249 in Canada) Suggested Retail Price $399 US

To order, call DELRINA direct...and ask for the "STEPS: For LANs $199 Special Offer"

*In the US, call* **1-408-363-2345 Ext. 242**

*In Canada, call* **1-416-441-3676 Ext. 305**

Applicable sales tax, shipping and handling not included.
Offer good until December 31, 1993, or while supplies last. Offer valid for one (1) copy per book.

● ● ● ● ● ● ● ● ● ● ● ● ● ● ● ● ● ● ● ● ● ● ● ● ● ● ● ● ● ● ● ● ● ● ● ● ● ● ● ● ● ● ● ● ● ● ● ● ● ● ● ● ● ● ●

In order to qualify for these software discounts, simply complete the registration form on the
facing page and return as directed. Then just call **MICROSOFT** or **DELRINA** directly to take
advantage of these special offers.

Please have the following ready when placing your order:

**METHOD OF PAYMENT** ☐ VISA ☐ Master Card ☐ AMEX

Card No.:_____

Card Holder Name:_____

Expiry Date:_____